MASTERING YOUR 5D SELF

"This wonderful book is a glimpse into Maureen's personal journey shared through messages from her spirit guides, insights from other light workers, and through practical guidance that helps us to navigate our journeys into a more awakened consciousness. Refreshingly honest and conversational, Maureen weaves her wisdom throughout its pages. Through her own deep life challenges, she exemplifies the inspiring message that no matter what hardships a person faces, with desire, heart, and the grace of spirit we can overcome them. At the heart of this book lies the message that each of us has the choice to change our destiny every day, to shift our perspectives, and to step more fully into an illuminated and joyful fifth-dimensional life."

Tricia McCannon, author of
Return of the Divine Sophia

"Maureen St. Germain continues to be on the leading edge. *Mastering Your 5D Self* provides new information and explanations to help ease your transformation and thrive in 5D. Learn how to access your chakras through your heart, reactivate your pineal gland, get deeper sleep, clear patterns that are holding you back, and much more. Uplifting and inspiring, I encourage you to read this book!"

Margaret (Peg) M. Donahue, founder of
Feng Shui Connections and
coauthor of *Money Is an Energy Game*

"This is the perfect guidebook to master the shift into 5D. Maureen has crafted an easy-to-read book full of fascinating and intriguing information, combined with relatable personal stories from her own life illustrating the principles. The book is full of guided meditations and easy-to-use tools to help you transform into 5D, manifesting your life into one of joy and flow and truly living your best life."

Anne Gordon de Barrigón, retreat success coach
at Whale and Dolphin Wisdom Retreats

"This book will help you navigate your journey in this intriguing new world of 5D. Maureen St. Germain gives clear, deep instructions and heartfelt descriptions of what to expect. She shows you that when you step into the full power of 5D your traditional ways of solving problems, dealing with issues and relationships, and your growth dramatically shift and transform. *Mastering Your 5D Self* is a must-read and *the* book to keep on your desk as an essential map for mastering your brilliant new life and way of being with the principles of unconditional love."

Sylvia Moss, vibrational sound healer,
spiritual teacher, and author
of *Angels of New York*

"In a world that sometimes seems confusing, chaotic, and even lost, Maureen offers hope. In her words, 'Many individuals have led lifetimes of compromise. They have been . . . complicit, because they didn't believe they had a choice.' But there is an alternative: 'Believe and know that you are free!' The answer lies in the fifth dimension—the 'Magnanimous Dimension.' This book is an antidote to what we too often hear in the evening news!"

Jim Willis, author of
The Quantum Akashic Field

"Stepping into the full power of 5D means giving up the traditional ways of dealing with problems, relationships, and personal growth. Maureen St. Germain shows us how to navigate this new terrain with grace and simplicity."

Debra Poneman, author of *Spiritual Leadership* and
founder of Yes to Success, Inc.

"A marvelous follow-up to *Waking Up in 5D, Mastering Your 5D Self* provides the reader with ways to explore more spiritual tools and transformative shortcuts, such as activating meditations, sound healing, and crystals, along with channeled wisdom and advanced insights from angels and other higher beings. I recommend it to all who follow the many paths of enlightenment."

Lynn Andrews, New York Times bestselling author
of the Medicine Woman series

"Filled with surprises and insightful explanations, you can now explore Maureen's unique understanding of the full power of 5D. What a powerful guide for humanity's evolution."

Lumari, creation catalyst, spiritual guide,
and multidimensional channel

MASTERING YOUR 5D SELF

Tools to Create a New Reality

MAUREEN J. ST. GERMAIN

Bear & Company
Rochester, Vermont

Bear & Company
One Park Street
Rochester, Vermont 05767
www.BearandCompanyBooks.com

Text stock is SFI certified

Bear & Company is a division of Inner Traditions International

Copyright © 2022 by Maureen J. St. Germain

All rights reserved. No part of this book may be reproduced or utilized in any form or by any means, electronic or mechanical, including photocopying, recording, or by any information storage and retrieval system, without permission in writing from the publisher.

Cataloging-in-Publication Data for this title is available from the Library of Congress

ISBN 978-1-59143-397-2 (print)
ISBN 978-1-59143-398-9 (ebook)

Printed and bound in the United States by Lake Book Manufacturing, Inc.
The text stock is SFI certified. The Sustainable Forestry Initiative® program promotes sustainable forest management.

10 9 8 7 6 5 4 3 2 1

Text design and layout by Virginia Scott Bowman
This book was typeset in Garamond Premier Pro with Hermann used as the display typeface

To send correspondence to the author of this book, mail a first-class letter to the author c/o Inner Traditions • Bear & Company, One Park Street, Rochester, VT 05767, and we will forward the communication, or contact the author directly at **www.maureenstgermain.com**.

The dedication is to you—

dear reader and experiencer . . .

This book is no magic pill. You must participate in your own learning. Let me help you by sharing what I have learned, and let the universe teach you like I've been taught. This book is about helping you acquire the knowledge you seek as you move from ways of learning and knowing to ways of being. Let me and others lead you; don't let us dictate. Undertake these practices because they resonate with you, and because they have worked for me and my students.

Claim your God victory. The God spark programmed you to self-discovery. Even though many generations before us have been slaves to systems, governments, biases, churches, and cultures, we are slaves no more. Claim this.

Believe and know that you are free!

Contents

Prologue

The Magnanimous Heart and the Magnanimous Dimension

This book is about the ongoing process of waking up in 5D and connecting the dots in a way that helps you be even more than you thought you could be! If you have read my book *Waking Up in 5D,* much of the material in the first section of this book will seem familiar. I wanted to give a little explanation for those who have not read the earlier book and at the same time not bore you with material you may already be familiar with. This book could be considered a follow-up to *Waking Up in 5D,* and though this book is valuable on its own, I encourage you to check out that book too, if you've not had a chance to read it yet.

The channeled message below came from Sanat Kumara and the Great Karmic Board, which is the overseer of this planet's evolution. Sanat Kumara is the great guru, savior of the Earth. He is known in all the major religions by various names: Ancient of Days, Skanda/Kartikkeya, Brahma-Sanam Kumara, and even for Sufi Muslims, the Green Man. He came to Earth from Venus with 144,000 volunteers to help "turn around" an errant mankind.

The channeled message that came through one day when I was meditating identified how humans might connect with a larger perspective that incorporates the views of others as well as their own. When called in by naming it, the Magnanimous Dimension, what it does is expand you into a fifth-dimensional perspective, which allows you to see both sides of the equation. Part of our "job" as emerging "Ascended Masters" (and yes, we're all becoming Ascended Masters!) is to find ways to embody the principles of unconditional love. These principles are magnified by calling in the Magnanimous Dimension.

Many of you have heard the phrase, "Most benevolent outcome." This has been popularized by an author whom you love, Tom T. Moore who has written several books on this subject, referring to it as the gentle way. It is well adopted by many, and rightly so. You now have the outcome, of the combined dimensions with you, and may ask for a *most magnanimous outcome!* Tom has been teaching about "the most benevolent outcome." This (Magnanimous Dimension) could be compared to that work, only far more expansive than one event or request because it makes it easy for you to be magnanimous without trying! Please know that all the masters and teachers are way-showers into your mastery. They give humans a "leg up" from what they may be likely to know or do.

So what exactly is 5D? How can we get there and what can we know about it? In the book *Waking Up in 5D* I disclosed that the easiest way to begin to understand 5D is to think of what the traditional churches call heaven. Start with that. Then think of some of your science fiction movies where a person manages to change their vibration and lands in a whole new world that is familiar, but significantly different. The good news is that many humans are already vibrating at fifth dimension. And yes, it is a vibrational shift, not a physical one, and even if humans do not recognize it as fifth dimension, it is true, they choose this frequency often.

You might also think of the dimensions like Russian dolls that are nested together. Interestingly, when you are at fifth dimension you can participate in third dimension, bringing "up" those around you. You may "play" in third dimension from fifth, but again, holding your fifth-dimensional vibration means you have no polarity, no judgment or bias. You may feel a preference for one thing over another but even that is mitigated by the "nonjudgmental" vibe of the fifth dimension. From this new vantage point (fourth or fifth dimension), you can experience the lower dimensions with grace, compassion, and dispassionate interest.

In *Waking Up in 5D* I delve into the dimensions, explaining their function and overarching purpose. In my book *Opening the Akashic Records* we are reminded that the higher dimensions are accessible through certain processes, and you can actually be multidimensional when you are channeling the Akashic Records from the eleventh dimension. Remember, 5D is a zone of unconditional love without polarity. It is also a way of being that is so powerful that its emanations change everything around it to unconditional love.

One of the great masters who oversees the Earth and her people is the Great Divine Director. His energy is constantly bathing the Earth to assist individuals in "remembering" their purpose, and aligning to the will of Source (or God). Because humanity has free will, it isn't always easy to make the highest and best choice, and asking for this high initiate's support will improve your chances of success with the least amount of effort. When you do not know what to do in any given situation, and choices seem good in all directions, asking the Great Divine Director to watch over you as you make your decision will ensure your success.

As mentioned earlier, Sanat Kumara is the great master who came to Earth to help mankind. Man's "inhumanity" to one another was so great it was felt by the Great Karmic Board that it would be better to allow the Earth to "self-destruct" rather than try to bring it back into alignment with the Divine. Sanat Kumara volunteered and then called for volunteers from among his followers to assist. They were tasked with holding light on the planet and in so doing, were able to make a positive impact on the situation. They succeeded. If you feel a connection to the number 144,000, you may have been one of those early volunteers from Venus.

As I was working on this book, in January of 2021, one of the certified Akashic Records guides channeled the following message:

JANUARY 16, 2021, ELLES TADDEO

The law of cause and effect used to be the incorrect interpretation of karmic laws. It has now been changed to the law of choice and effect, which indicates the responsibility is with the chooser. At any time a new choice may be made that can strengthen or override the effect of the previous choice. All choices are inseparably attached to a result. With the changeover from "cause" to "choice," karma, as it has been interpreted through the last two thousand years, in a sense does not exist anymore. The new interpretation is taking effect slowly as new insights are gained and the veil of darkness disappears. Humans will gradually become stronger and more willing to accept responsibility for their choices because those choices will be recognized as God choices. As the dark veil disappears, the truth becomes more and more clear. It is possible *NOW!* The switch can be made instantaneously. We bless you and love you.

Who are you?

We are the Lords of Time and Karma. We love you and support you. Go in peace. All is well.

THE NINE. CHANNELED IN AUGUST 2020.

Who are the nine? They are an exquisite, loving, creative energy emanating from Source, the sun behind the sun. They represent the love and delight that can be best understood as resource of Creation.*

*To elaborate, the Council of Nine are the major representatives of the Great Blue Lodge of the Great Blue Light. This Great Blue Light of Creation comes directly from Lord Siraya. It first passes through the Council of the Nine and from there is distributed to the High Light Councils of Orion. From there, it passes through all the great sacred councils of archangels, angels, Elohim, and Time Lords (the lineage of heaven) that exist in all of Creation.

We bring you a message of hope and love. Yours is a trying time and prayer is the ability to stay tuned to the Divine. We bring you love and light. Maureen is our messenger in this moment. Maureen has been our messenger all along, yet did not want to appear to be so different as to be rejected. Maureen, your heart is open wide; you are our channel and you can and will be both loved and rejected. Get used to it.

Now for our message for you to scribe this day. Think of your most evolved messenger. Think of the people you listen to and work with. Each one can be compelling and interesting. So many people can be in the dark, not being able to discern their own thoughts from the overlay that would confuse. Many fail to see or understand their true purpose in Creation. *We* know, *you* see. You have insisted that you remain in your beloved New York. We *know* how much you love this city, and certainly you will be supported through this time of great prosperity as well as evolution.

We are here to help humanity and to help you. We are emanating through you to create a bigger awareness and understanding of the importance of light and love on the planet. So many can see that the world is not right. So many can see that there is much work to be done.

You may proceed.

Use this time [of difficulty] to be diligent, focused, holy, and sincere. There are many individuals who will not be able to adjust. You have adjusted well and continue to be serving humanity well.

Can we talk about the Magnanimous Dimension?

Yes, as indicated by us, we have urged you to bring in the energy of the combined integration of three dimensions. We know you are quite familiar with the energy of the third dimension, its polarity, its divisiveness, its goodness, and yes there is goodness in the third dimension. Fourth dimension is integrating now within each of you. You are beginning to tap into the depths of joy, presence, and love. Fourth dimension is the portal through which you magnify and transport yourself into fifth dimension. Because your world has been slow to catch up, we now are offering to you this combined quality of this nexus into the fifth dimension to reach each and every one of you. We name it the "Magnanimous Dimension," an energy of great integration. It consists of knowing and understanding the perils of third, the passion of fourth, the ecstasy of fifth, and distilling it into an exquisite elixir of magnanimousness. You now have with you the outcome of the combined dimensions, and you may ask for a *most magnanimous outcome!*

THE NINE. CHANNELED IN AUGUST 2020.

Your choice of words matters greatly. There are many phrases you can add to your vocabulary so you are always ready to keep the conversation at optimum. What have I "ordered" from the universe today? The universe must know something I don't know because . . . or I wonder how that will come out? I'll let the angels show me how really good they are. God bless it. I am so grateful for *everything* coming my way! Or my friend Tracy's phrase: *It's all divine.*

There are many modern-day mystics, and some have been way ahead of their time. The following quote is from an oft-vilified lecturer and philanthropist. He righted his mistakes and stepped up into integrity after abandoning his family and repaying his in-laws for supporting his first wife. It's not easy to be a hero, and some of the most unlikely heroes are bad guys who step up. Think of the amazing stories of Neale Donald Walsch of *Conversations with God* fame.

> We can choose to be audacious enough to take responsibility for the entire human family. We can choose to make our love for the world be what our lives are really about. Each of us now has the opportunity, the privilege, to make a difference in creating a world that works for all of us. It will require courage, audacity, and heart. It is much more radical than a revolution—it is the

beginning of a transformation in the quality of life on our planet. You have the power to fire the shot heard 'round the world.'*

JANUARY 3, 2020

The Great Divine Director and Sanat Kumara
Channeled by Maureen St. Germain

This is the Great Divine Director, along with Sanat Kumara. Sanat Kumara will be doing all of the talking. The Great Divine Director's presence is to provide the great matrix, which we will talk about in a moment.

We ask you to look at your upcoming events in your life with a renewed sense of wonder. Let it be for your highest and best good. Let it be fun and easy. You are going to need to let go of many things. Some of those things you might say, "No—I must have that—I must have that." And we say, well, see if you can find a substitute for that. See if you can find another way to get that need met. Or perhaps find that you don't need it and let it go.

We point you to the concept of death and say to you when someone dies, you immediately think about your loss and what you have lost. And we say to you, what if you thought about all of the good that came from this person being in your life? What if you allowed yourself to move into deep gratitude that you had the ability to be with this person for so very long? Maureen's mother used to always focus on the gratitude when her friends would complain about paying high taxes. She would say, "I am so grateful that we have the money. I grew up poor." When she talked about Maureen's father being a prisoner of war, Maureen's mother identified that it was a miracle that he came back alive—so many did not. And that they were given all these years.

*Werner Erhard, "Creating a World That Works for Everyone," *Graduate Review,* February 1980. Werner Hans Erhard (born John Paul Rosenberg; September 5, 1935) is an American author and lecturer best known for founding est, which operated from 1971 to 1984. He has written, lectured, and taught on self-improvement.

So no matter what you had that you have now lost, we ask you to start counting the blessings that came from the having of this thing, and we ask you to look around you. All of Earth, all of humanity, is asking you to live on less, to live more simply, to have more time for contemplation, more time for yourself. To look at the things that you have lost or are losing, with equanimity and compassion for yourself.

Each one of you has your own path and your own burden. Each one of you is facing some losses, some bigger than others. Your need to compare yourself with others is unnecessary. We propose that you use the human nature of comparison to think about all of the good that you have received. When you are focused in the present, saying to yourself, "Yes, but I am so missing this person or this thing," say, "Well, I am so grateful that I came to depend upon this. I am so grateful that I had this experience."

Keep in mind that your heart will be broken. Keep in mind that you will continue to lose. Keep in mind that you will get through this. Do not force yourself to move through the grieving of your losses. Instead, allow. Allow the grieving to go deep, and then come out of it. Again, go deep and come out of it. And like a sine wave that has a high and low of lesser and lesser proportions, we suggest to you that you are easing away from that which you have lost. Be fruitful and kind. Do not suffer over your suffering. One way to make sure that you keep this in balance is to count how many times you tell your sad story. Make it no more than three times. If you know your sister will give you a little more attention over a lost job or the end of a relationship, then don't tell it to the first person that comes along, but wait until your sister calls you. We hope you see the humor here.

We also want you to know that you need to use your tools. Your tools can consist of the essential oils, your crystals, and your special disks, your tools such as tapping, and of course asking us for assistance—asking us for enough help to get you through this. You do not need to do anything alone anymore. You will never be alone anymore. Even if you have lost your beloved, you will not be alone. We will not abandon you. We will stand close by waiting for you to ask us for help. Maureen likes to say, "Imagine a room full of servants standing around. And you finally say to them, 'What are you doing just standing around?' And they say, 'We are waiting for your direction. We are waiting for you to tell us what you want. We are waiting to hear your heart's desire.'"

If you feel sadness in your heart, we ask you to go watch sunsets. We gave this directive to Maureen when she went through a big grief many, many years ago. Since then she found a scientific study that clearly establishes sunsets actually help take you out of a depression. Do your meditations. Ask for your day of heaven on earth. Ask! Only by asking can you receive what you need.

You may be called upon to counsel someone else who has experienced loss. And we say to you, let that loss be shared. Listen, offer no judgment, nor feedback—just listen. That will be enough. And after you have listened to their sad story, you can say, "Can I offer a little prayer, right now, out loud with you?" And your companion may say, "Yes." And if they do, you simply say, "We are asking for all the angels and the beings of light to assist you in moving through and resolving this sadness or grief, your feelings of loss, so that I can step into my place of power, my place of true neutrality, of unconditional love for life."

Now the Great Divine Director wishes to address this ideal of your great (divine) matrix, and to alert you that although it is a matrix, it is a living field, which means it can shift and change. And we ask you to ask the Divine Director to overlay his electronic presence over you, to enliven your divine matrix so that following your divine matrix is fun and easy; to put it in neon, to ask your angels to help you notice. In this way you will become fully aligned with your divine plan. As you become fully aligned with your divine plan, you are the solution. And we remind you that healing you is part of the solution. When you heal your heart and expand your heart's energy, you influence the world around you. When you influence the world around you, you expand your influence again. As you shift and change, allow others to help you. Allow your otherworldly helpers to help you. Ask your Higher Self to step in and assist you. And know that we will never leave you. We will never leave you. I am Sanat Kumara with the Great Divine Director.

SANAT KUMARA AND THE GREAT DIVINE DIRECTOR

JUNE 25, 2020

Message from Great Divine Director

We are here with you to assist you in understanding all the mysteries that are piling up around, and your work.

There are forces at hand that have agendas that are out of sync with the version of the reality that shows humans making their transformational shifts. We ask you to allow yourself to get comfortable, happy, and joyous, and this will prevent them from succeeding. So even though there is a drama all around you, even though there are rules and regulations that you may not like, we say to you, especially in America, that those rules are *not* part of the plan and those are persons who believe they have authority, but they do not.

Little by little, the people all around you are waking up and discovering that they are being ordered around by those that do not have that authority.

We ask you to find your own place in that. If you are not a warrior, do not pick up that sword. If you are a warrior and it is your delight to do this, then do it with passion, love, and compassion. Do not pick up the sword to be fierce or to fight. This could cause you to catch the energy of anger and hatred that is being projected into the reality to cause mankind to hate one another and bounce you back into the polarity energy of 3D.

This energy is no longer supported,* and we, from our vantage point, are doing our best to disband that energy, to dilute that energy, to antidote that energy. We ask you to notice when you see

*Think of this like being told that Windows XP is no longer supported. You can keep using that software, but we prefer you upgrade.

chemtrails in the sky or you feel other energies working against you. For instance, if you walk into a place and the energies feel dark, simply ask for the energies of the Angelic Realm. Ask for the energies to immediately be transmuted and transformed for the highest and best good of those present, and for the highest and best good of the people coming behind you, so there is absolutely no drama.

You are a magician. You have the power within you and you are being woken up to the fact that you have this power and that you *can* make a difference. You may think that you must do certain things. Certainly there are reasons to respond with compliance in certain situations. The reason for compliance is not because you must but because you know you will attract attention to yourself that you don't want, or you wish to use love to disarm the battle from a different vantage point.

All of these responses are appropriate. We remind you again, you have absolute power, and you can and will stand up and be counted for your work as a spiritual being; for those prayers for the leaders who are exposed to the liars and the lies and their action. We ask you to be filled with compassion, no matter what!

If this were your son or daughter who was the guilty party of whatever you hear about, you would ask for compassion. You would ask for the courts to be merciful. Be merciful for the transformation of the society. Not for those who would have you fail—not so they could continue their drama or continue their wounding of humans. But to be merciful toward them in a way that says you do not require they have a level of suffering that is greater than what they have inflicted. Your sense of justice at this time is understandable. Your sense of fair play is understandable. But in order to step out of this 3D matrix you must unhook from your need to *know* that justice was served. Know that those who are handling this situation are handling it with ease and they are working on releasing this bondage of keeping score, this bondage of holding humanity in a place of control to control the drama, to control judgment, or to control the outcome.

We say to you, "Find your joy." Find a way to be in your joy, every single day. We say to you, if you are not a warrior, this is *not* your battle. If you are a warrior and you are ready to do battle you will have support from the universe. Do not go off on your own. You must have a support system in 3D and from us. Your efforts will be counted. If you follow your own guidance you will know those times that you are to step up and you will know those times that you are to stand down.

The most important thing is to stay in your joy. The second most important thing is to allow yourself to look at those situations, those crimes you are learning about, and realize that justice will be served in whatever way justice is served and you do not have to raise your voice on this. Nor do you have to use your energy to cry foul or employ any other statement that judges this outcome as unfair to some and not to others.

We remind you of the message from Sanat Kumara who said, "The game (of 3D) is over when there are no more players. Will you be the first to leave or the last?" We remind you and we ask you to make an active effort every day to look at the news, look at the information, and then pull back, unhook from it, and decide that it is all theater. Decide what you will decide without the moving for judgment, without moving into anger or frustration, and to be proactive and powerful and in your joy. We want you to understand you *are* powerful, and you *can* control your circumstances.

This is the Great Divine Director. I hold the love and light around the planet. As some of you know, my causal body is larger than the Earth. I will help you. Call upon me daily. Those of you who have studied the Akashic Records with Maureen St. Germain know to call me every day. We will help you. We are the team of Ascended Masters who support this planet and are part of the great body of beings who are supporting humanity's transformation.

Stay ready and aware to those who are waking up. Do not put your agenda on anyone. Instead, wait for the request to come to you. We remind you that your situation could get worse before it gets better. Your choosing to stay steady will help others to stay steady. We ask you to pick up the Divine Government meditation (free) from Maureen's website and do that daily if you can. Many

> of you have waited a long time for this victory. It is just around the corner. We are with you always. And you are never alone. That is all.
>
> THE GREAT DIVINE DIRECTOR

In stepping into higher consciousness you may find that these twelve recognitions will help you identify your path and your way through life.

If you are looking for a simple set of rules to guide your progress, you might enjoy using these twelve concepts for mastering your fifth-dimensional self.

1. Believe in the Higher Self and learn to activate it and use it. For many years I have been sharing this simple, straightforward method of connecting to your Higher Self. This connection is to the higher version of you. It is not better than you, nor do you let it rule you. Like a good coach it can see beyond where you can see and can guide you in making decisions that will give you your highest and best outcome.
2. Recognize that your Higher Self can guide you home. Your Higher Self is you, and knows what you planned for yourself before you came into this body. Your Higher Self has access to your past, and also your current goals and desires. Nothing can stand in your way of knowing the highest and best choice when you have developed this Higher Self connection.
3. Recognize the benefit of asking your Higher Self about everything. This simple concept becomes super obvious when you are in the forty-five-day practice mode of Higher Self training. After your forty-five-day practice, you might choose to not follow your Higher Self. Once you ask your Higher Self about an action to take, and then choose a different action, the bypassed Higher Self option will be recognized as the better one at some point after the action has occurred. This will often make you laugh, as many a student has ruefully reported, "I *knew* better, but I did it anyway." A few of these "missteps" will make you understand that even when it is counterintuitive you can benefit from following your Higher Self's

suggestion. Remember you have free will. Your commitment to follow your Higher Self all the time is still based on choice!

4. Be willing to take a blow to the heart. A blow to the heart is when someone who is close to you, someone you love and cherish and who you believe is on the same path or wavelength as you, does something you would not do. It challenges your safety, and your feelings of trust, because it catches you completely by surprise. A blow to the heart is described in detail in *Beyond the Flower of Life*. Knowing how to recognize a blow to the heart becomes a powerful tool to raise your consciousness. Choosing to "love them anyway" in such occasions breaks a barrier to the "love" you have in your heart (conditional, expectation based), and helps you move into a higher plane of consciousness. This is not to suggest you should put up with abuse. A blow to the heart from a friend may cause the friend to move down in status to acquaintance. Let that be okay.
5. Recognize that you are the cocreator of your reality. Almost every spiritual teacher will tell you this, but it is truly difficult to accept when things are not going the way you want them to. "Accepting" that you are cocreator means that every part of you, your Higher Self, your oversoul, and the human you, are collaborating to produce opportunities for growing your spiritual self. Your oversoul is that compilation of expressions of you (in many realities) that oversees the many expressions of you.
6. Recognize that you can change this reality at will. This is another concept that although widely taught, is difficult to accept, let alone utilize. God-mastery is the goal of becoming fifth dimensional. The tools in this book are offered to show you how very powerful you are and invite you to practice as a true master of your destiny.
7. Recognize that the way you receive is not related to the giver. As you mature, this principle is fairly obvious. You begin to understand that others do not think the way you do, and they are "doing the best they can." Amazingly, as you move into spiritual mastery in fifth dimension you lose the need to know why people do what they do, and instead find yourself moving into compassion for the

foibles of others. As a fifth-dimensional being, you can prepare to be amazed every day!

8. Recognize that all individuals are on their own journey. Each and every human is a God free being. Some people are afraid to make mistakes, which is why they follow the teachings and beliefs of others rigidly. The other (expert) has made pontifications and promises that their path will solve your problems and bring you peace. Peace comes from within, and your journey means that you include yourself and others, expressing unconditional love that moves beyond the need to know "why" and instead moves into a greater understanding of "what" is really going on. This is one of the primary uses of opening the Akashic Records for yourself. You begin to understand a much larger picture of your life and the interactions of others. For example, a devout meditating man seeking understanding of his young adult daughter's abuse and disrespect toward him, learned from the Record Keepers through me, that he and his daughter were adversaries in a previous lifetime. He went on to advance spiritually. She did not. He agreed to sponsor her in this lifetime. She still sees him as her adversary.

   The Record Keepers further advised him that this would take time, that she would "come around" as a loving daughter and his job was to "love her anyway" until that happened. And then they added that it could take a few years! As a parent, I can say that although that information is helpful, it isn't exactly what he had hoped to hear! On the other hand, the Record Keepers assured him that it wasn't a "debt owed," but a choice he made out of love and compassion at higher levels of existence, and here on Earth his job is to—to love her anyway, which helped him advance spiritually as well!

9. Recognize that you are the center of your universe. You make an amazing discovery when you realize that you are in control of your feelings and thoughts and your reactions to others, and that you are not entitled to anything with respect to others. This leads to self-mastery. When you begin to realize that what others think or do makes no difference unless you let it, you will be the center of your universe.

10. Recognize that each day you have a clean slate. This discovery is a beautiful explanation of "no more Karma" as detailed in *Waking Up in 5D,* chapter 4. It means that the errors of yesterday (which you usually regret at some point) cannot hold you back. You may "learn" to make new choices that do not hold "leanings" toward the misbehavior, thoughts, or words that you now regret! It also means you can forgive yourself each night knowing that the next day you get to start over, and that "keeping score" on yourself beyond inner awareness to do better tomorrow is all that is needed! This clears that "not good enough" energy that may overtake you at times.
11. Recognize that you have an obligation to operate in integrity. Just because there is no more karma does not mean you can keep doing the same inappropriate thing day after day. It means that you own your choices, recognize where or how you could be different, and then choose another way the next time you encounter a similar situation. It also means you *get it* that you have a personal duty to yourself to hold yourself to the high standards you hold for others. Finally, it means that your thoughts, words, and deeds match and accurately reflect your beliefs, words, and deeds. A funny way to understand this is to say, "I'm trying to lose weight," then you go and eat donuts. You get the idea.
12. Be willing to stay connected to your Higher Self. This is a simple task but it takes a strong commitment to stay connected. It means you are willing to "check in" with your Higher Self daily on actions and decisions you will choose. Adults usually have well-developed egos that help them make decisions based on their history and understanding of the reality. When you engage with your Higher Self on a regular basis, you will find your Higher Self occasionally directing you in a counterintuitive way. Following the guidance of your Higher Self takes commitment and practice. Ultimately, this practice will lead you to higher and better outcomes than you could ever imagine.

Recently I received the following insights on fear from my very loving and sharing friend Tracy Jo.

Maureen, I just wanted to share this with you because I read your last article on fear. I have come to understand that fear is but another illusion to render one powerless to take action, any action necessary to overcome whatever the believed false fear is appearing as. We are not victims in this adventure of co-creation. We are a reflection of God or Source and I cannot find it anywhere within my being to logically or intuitively believe God is either fearful or a victim. So therefore, it would mean that I too—if I am willing to do the work to overcome myself (the illusion) and to understand who I truly am (God incarnate)—would never need to be a vehicle for fear. I am a Temple for God, a place where we (God and myself) can enter into together and commune with one another here in this world. Fear cannot enter here, for if I allow it in, my connection/communion is temporarily severed and, is it not the goal to walk in connection with our Creator as One all the time? Albert Einstein said: "I want to know the mind of God, everything else is just details." I ponder the Mind of God often and have wondered could all or any of this creation have happened, had He been fearful in any way? My heart tells me no. Jesus said repeatedly many, many times "Fear Not," and so as I consider him to be one of my Master teachers. I take his advice and I ask others to do the same. Fear not and Love more! I believe the antidote for fear is LOVE, and it starts by Loving yourself and knowing you have within your very DNA the antidote. And when you realize that you are the antidote, which is LOVE, you will never fear that you are anything less ever again.

Fear is a messenger. It is asking you to notice if you are "replaying" someone else's directive or belief system. Or is it asking you to notice if you are out of alignment with your own beliefs? Fear asks you to change your belief or change your behavior. Finally, there is fear of fear. This is perpetuated by certain energies that are on a mission to control you. When you feel fear be sure to ask yourself, "What am I afraid of?" This will help you dispel myths, desire more information, and create an awareness of the thoughts of others that may be influencing you and an awareness of your own thoughts. Later in this book you will learn more about what the Lords of Time have to say about fear.

1

Why Are We Here?

The short answer is, we are here to expand the database. We separated from that which is *inseparable* in order to experience more than we already were. If we were already everything, we would not be able to experience "not-God." Because we created a system that made it okay to select the "not-God" choice, we increase the possible experiences of Source. Now, however, it is time to rein in the "children" who have become so caught up in the game of polarity that they do not remember who they really are. The game itself has gone too far and too deep for it to continue, so the grand experiment is now complete.

The answer of why we are here is not just singular. It is important to understand that there are many kinds of people who have incarnated here on Earth. Each group will have its own reason to be here.

DIFFERENT GROUPS ON THE PLANET AT THIS TIME

Let's start with the travelers. The travelers have the dispensation to travel throughout the universe. The only injunction is to be curious about where they land, and to make sure they leave the place better than they found it. The best example of this is found in the movie *K-Pax,* a delightful story about a person who appears in Grand Central Station, New York City, amid a crowd of people. His claim is that he is from a place called K-Pax. These travelers are curious about the way life exists in other places, and may not interfere, unless their presence improves things. This may be a bit difficult to understand, so watching the movie may awaken your perception of this interaction without interference.

Another group is the way-showers, who are similar to the guardians. The way-showers are evolved beings who have earned the right to be teachers and helpers of the people of Earth. They have incarnated many times on Earth and have achieved a level of devotion and mastery. Many are members of the 144,000 souls who came to Earth with the Ascended Master Sanat Kumara when Earth was at her darkest hour. Many of the 144,000 souls are back in embodiment now. Their devotion to the Ascended Master Sanat Kumara, also known as Ancient of Days, and to the light, is overriding in them. They are good people and their purpose is to show up. Sometimes only their presence is required.

The next group I'd like to refer to is the souls of the Earth who are here as guardians and helpers. Like the way-showers, they too have come to be of service to humankind. The guardians are different from way-showers because their mission is to serve the teachers and other spiritual leaders and help keep them safe. This means they may have regular jobs and show up for special events. They have a strong need to "keep an eye on things." This might mean being the beloved or partner of a spiritual teacher or their benefactor. They could be the student of the teacher and find a way to always be on the lookout for the person they are meant to guard. Many spiritual teachers have guardians in their lives. The teacher might not even know who they are, or their capacity as guardians.

The group that is being cared for by all these beautiful helpers are those who are "regulars" on Earth; they are working toward their own mastery. This group is composed of Earth humans who are ready to be evolved, and now are ready to "wake up." Their purpose is to wake up.

Finally, there is a very special group of souls who are already Ascended Masters in embodiment and who are here as helpers and way-showers as well. However, their role is leadership in many cases. They have extraordinary skills, compassion, and understanding. They usually have many skills and can do almost anything they put their mind to.

Their job is to provide leadership and to ensure that the human race continues to evolve and move well beyond the dangers humanity faces in the first half of the twenty-first century. Many are not able to access past lives in their spiritual quests, as those records have been sealed. In addition, one of their most striking qualities is that they are fearless. If you are a parent of one of these masters, you must learn to listen to your Higher Self, to know what kind of guidance and discipline you are to provide. It isn't easy parenting an Ascended Master because they do not "need" childhood. It is simply a means to get to adulthood, where they show up as leaders and changemakers.

Remember, if you are hearing an inner voice that tells you that you "should" do something, it's coming from your left brain, the logical part of the brain. This is because "should" is not part of an inner guidance and intuition process. If you have a strong feeling that the information floated in or "landed" in your brain, then you are very likely receiving from the intuitive side of the brain. Always check with your Higher Self as to what your best course of action should be as a parent to these children who are already Ascended Masters.

A CRISIS POINT FOR EACH OF YOU

Many of you have been or are in crisis. You've worried how you will survive and get through the crisis you are experiencing. Now is the time to step up and let the crisis cause you to activate your gifts. These gifts may have remained dormant for a very long time. In choosing how to explain your past difficulties, you might prefer to say "I have transformed myself" instead of "I am a cancer survivor!" When you focus on fear (such as the cancer in our example), you give up your power to a powerful force. Instead, focus on the present now. Wondering why something happened to you means you are trying to validate where you *were* instead of attracting what you need now in the present. Wondering why you are jinxed will only validate and attract more drama.

We are on the cusp of this fantastic metamorphosis of humanity, ergo the phoenix. The phoenix is found in Japanese, Russian, Egyptian, and Native American traditions. The phoenix is often related to the sun; exists as a single, powerful, benevolent, beautiful, and melodic giant bird that can live for thousands of years; and according to legend, births its replacement from the ashes of its burning nest. We are seeing many things around us that we know cannot last—the old way of doing or thinking of things—and we must completely "burn these out of our system" to make room for something much better.

One big example is the problem of plastics. Many organizations are on the cutting edge of eliminating the problem from our oceans. There are almost 250 cities nationwide with some kind of a ban on plastics; New York City is the second city in the nation to ban one-use plastics (like straws). Each year, around 8 million metric tons of plastic enter the world's oceans, the equivalent of one full garbage truck every minute!

Humanity is full of problem solvers, creative thinkers, researchers, and others who rely on their intuition and dreamtime to come up with fabulous solutions. *You should too!* When you actively choose this, you can "Wake up in 5D." This leads to "knowing" without knowing why or how you know. This is the creative process of inventors of the past. Consciously choosing to be part of the solution is to remove the blinders (of not caring about the end result . . . like what happens to the trash in the landfill). This is truly what free will is all about. The act of choosing easily engages you in your 5D self. It's even easier with an activated MerKaBa. The MerKaBa is an energetic star-tetrahedronal field that you build by yourself for yourself. There are planetary MerKaBas as well. This shape, once activated, produces the most evolved expression of a living thing, even it if hasn't become that most evolved being. Perhaps you could explain it as a uniform that automatically makes you fifth dimensional effortlessly.

Any gardener knows that a well-trimmed plant or tree yields more fruit than one that has not been trimmed. As a child growing up on a farm, I learned this lesson firsthand. Your own practice of meditation fine-tunes your budding abilities and allows you to yield more fruit of wisdom and understanding of the world around you. Your meditation practices fine-tune you to your true divine self.

So how do we change?

First, we begin to realize there is a problem that we need to stop contributing to. This occurs because global awareness grows within individuals and countries deciding they no longer wish to participate in the problem. Then we change slowly.

Let's take another look at the issue of plastics. Fortunately, there are many organizations that are creating real solutions to the plastics problem! One such example is 4Ocean. This organization is actively cleaning and promoting ocean cleanup. When you let go of your belief systems about anything, such as how valuable plastics have been to modern man and now, since humanity has created a big problem for the oceans with our plastic waste, we "recalibrate." Once you recalibrate, it is noticeable to you and others, and humanity can choose ways to move away from how we formerly used plastics and find new ways to eliminate the waste.

RECALIBRATION: ANOTHER FORM OF LETTING GO

Sometimes we want to control things because we do not feel safe. This is understandable in a world where child abuse and dysfunctional families exist. Certainly, all of us are control freaks to varying degrees! When my children were little, I wanted them to put the catsup in a certain spot in the fridge where I could see when we were getting low. Families with children know what a staple catsup can be, and being on a budget, I didn't want to purchase it sooner than needed.

Education is responsibility. I make it my personal responsibility. As I learn, I choose to support projects that help us take steps toward the welfare of the Earth. Mother Earth is my home and I desire to help her "get well." As you let go of your treasured belongings, treasured habits and patterns, give yourself permission to "rise from the ashes of your own funeral pyre" with a renewed optimism and expectation of a marvelous future.

As you face your own dramas of not enough, how you approach "not enough" will improve your success. What if you moved into wonder? I wonder where the money will come from to cover the rent? You don't ask yourself expecting an immediate answer, but pose the question as if your unseen helpers and the matrix of your life will produce the answer.

You do not have to know how this will work out. When you move into wonder you give the universe something to work with—because you've moved into solution energy. I wonder how I can get more out of my life? I wonder how I will get this project done? Consider multiple solutions. Brainstorm with others, and let all restraint be removed. Let the universe surprise you. If you feel you are facing an inevitable situation with no other solution, make up a story about a version of your drama where a new solution appeared unexpectedly and produced an outcome that surprised you. Pretend you are the superhero. Tell yourself, "I expect to be amazed."

Many individuals have led lifetimes of compromise. They have been compromised, or complicit, because they didn't believe they had a choice. They have participated unknowingly in versions of reality that have slowed their progress. Consider that there could be another version of reality that occurs simultaneously that does not contain these difficulties. These multiple realities could play out pain and suffering and you could jump tracks into a version that is less painful. These multiple scenarios interact with your awareness like rippling water and can influence you unknowingly.

You are one of many souls who are ready and willing to step into their true God nature. Reading this book makes you one of them. Remember that you have many helpers waiting to assist—just ask your angels and guides! There are many ETs of the light here on the planet who have made the decision to return home at the end of this cycle and will not need to be going through Earth's Ascension program, even though they are here to help. In addition, there are many Ascended Masters who are already here, in human bodies, assisting the transformation of humanity by holding space for the humans who are ready to move up.

Humanity is going through a great reset. Some individuals have chosen to be part of a new Earth where they will get the opportunity of choosing, without the dark overlay that was planted to confuse and obfuscate. You may think you understand what is going on but I'd like to offer an umbrella metaphor. We often use logic to try to help ourselves process information that makes no sense. In the world of psychotherapy this is called cognitive dissonance. We see or experience one thing and then later we discover it was something else.

USING THE UMBRELLA METAPHOR TO UNDERSTAND LOGIC

Imagine you are looking outside your hotel room window in an urban area and seeing umbrellas unfurled. It must be raining, you say to yourself. But it's not dark! But if you are in Taiwan, you might realize the umbrellas are to block the sun shining brightly. And if you were in Hong Kong during the riots of 2019, you would think of an umbrella as a shield against tear gas . . . and stay inside! Umbrellas have one well-known use, and several alternate uses that we don't normally think of. Choosing to allow for solutions that you had not thought of opens up the opportunity to co-create beyond your typical way of understanding the universe.

As you learn to anchor your fifth-dimensional energy into your life, you are learning that *choosing* is the operative word. Fifth dimension is choosing to change before it is needed, before pain, suffering, or getting stuck! Resistance produces discomfort and often pain.

I have been rushed to the emergency room four times since my previous book *Waking Up in 5D* came out. Long before COVID, I was struggling with breathing! It's not pretty. I was suffering from a mold infestation so deep inside my lungs that it intensified every time I was near anything with mold: the eucalyptus tree near my house that has black mold coexisting on it, the rental car that had unseen mold, and the first and nearly fatal instance, which was mold in the air ducts of the classroom in the old building where I was teaching!

A couple of times I passed out and woke up intubated. My doctors thought it was COPD, or asthma, or some other lung disease. I kept telling them it was mold . . . however the forty or so blood tests they ordered didn't show "that" mold. Why do I tell you this? My guidance was clear, yet I couldn't get anyone to believe me! For years afterward I carried an EpiPen and used it in case the unthinkable happened. Now that my immune system is strong I have even more to be grateful for. I truly know what it is like to leave your body because you cannot breathe!

I've had (anaphylactic) episodes in foreign countries, on jets crossing the Atlantic, and other places far from home. Plenty of times it was so hard to physically get air into my lungs and breathe that I would have given up, yet I was fortunate to have amazing help from a remote healer who worked tirelessly on me using Quantum Energetics. Quantum Energetics Structured Therapy works to systematically clear the human blueprint (etheric body) of disruptions, catalyzing the client to regenerate, repatterning the physical in wellness. Practitioners study for years to learn a detailed system of corrective procedures for directing energies to clear from conditions such as fractures, swellings, and misalignments—for bones, organs, muscles, and organisms, working at the quantum level. I wouldn't be here today if it weren't for that healing help from Elizabeth T.

When you have a number of near-death experiences, such as I had with these events, it changes you. In moments like that, it is easy to think, *Maybe I'll just give up.* Even though I worked through this, it is totally scary today remembering that I was ready to give up. When you find breathing so difficult, thinking of escape dominates your thoughts.

There are a few of you amazing light bearers and healers who helped me hold it together. I would not be here without your help! This includes the group of healers at Edgar Cayce's Association for Research and Enlightenment Health Center who focused so much light on me that first time, I recovered briefly before the ambulance carted me off, and Carol K., incredible craniosacral healer and magical remote healer. Terri Young called in her team, Angels and the Serendipities, for boosts through some serious difficulty that was a close call and occurred while I was in China.

THE IMPORTANCE OF SHOWING UP

Like many of you may have also experienced, the difficulties seemed so huge that there were days I just didn't want to do anything! Yet I kept "showing up," teaching and holding classes because there were always signs and opportunities to tell me that it would "all work out." Amazingly, sometimes when I was physically sick I would be fully okay enough at class time to then fall apart between sessions. My inner realm teachers such as El Morya, St. Germain, and the Great Divine Director have always been there for me. I don't have all the answers. I am a way-shower. It is my desire to assist you to show the way.

Early in my career I lost everything I had valued: my marriage, my job, money, and eventually my house (that I thought was my retirement!). Each time I was sure "this" was the end, something would happen that would convince me that it was going to be okay and that I would go on to better things.

You may be feeling that at times. Know that life is totally worth living. Some of the individuals who have exited at their own hand have come through me to announce, "When I took my own life I was trying to hurt my wife." You cannot hurt anyone but yourself by letting go and giving up. The Record Keepers have articulated to more than one client of mine that if they overwhelmingly "want to go back home" then they probably aren't doing the job they came to do! Keep asking your angels and guides, "What can I do to help?" On my website there are free meditations that may assist you with this. One wonderful free meditation is the Divine Government meditation. You can also play it on SoundCloud.

Find a way to do the service you came to do. Learn to connect with your Higher Self so that you can learn the skill or skills that will help prepare you for the work you will do. Even if you do nothing else, the Higher Self Connection will help you know what you need to know. Study with the teachers beneficial to you, and they will help you know when you need to know your next steps. The six weeks' investment of time (to learn your Higher Self Connection) is a small price to pay for the gift that will be with you for the rest of your life. Then you can keep checking in with your Higher Self. Is it in my highest and best good to do this job? Read this book? Take this course? Study with this teacher?

While you are doing the job you came to do, you are filled with so much love that you become unstoppable. This is how you know you ARE doing what you came to do! Yes, each of us who are doing the job we came to do are all filled with so much light that nothing can stop us. We are collectively unstoppable as well, you and I. I need you, and hopefully you'll agree you need me. We are all in this together! Life will go on, and we will emerge from this birth canal into the great Golden Age we have always wanted. It hasn't always been easy, but it certainly is worthwhile.

You might be saying that bad stuff happens, and sure, situations and events can affect you. You don't like it. I say, you don't *have* to like it—but you might want to decide it won't control you. When you feel emotions that are loosely labeled as fear, resentment, anxiety, or anger, you get to choose what happens next.

FEAR, ANXIETY, AND RESENTMENT

Science has been able to tell us some pretty significant things about the emotions of fear and anxiety. Fear is the real danger of a physical threat; anxiety is the presumed danger of a perceived threat! Fear is a physical response and causes you to act, take steps to escape, or do battle. Anxiety is an emotional response that may cause you to slow down.

Neuroscientists tell us that fear and anxiety are distinct in the brain and begin with changes in the amygdala, an almond-shaped organ in the center of the brain. The importance of its shape is related to the vesica picscis, that shape found by identical-sized circles intersecting on the perimeter of the other. This shape is believed to be the source of life and written about extensively in books on sacred geometry. These two emotions physically stem from different receptors and are produced by different centers and chemicals in the brain. They stimulate both autonomic and nonautonomic response.

This is important to understand because both are perversions of "time" and are based on our ability to remember or to project and have nothing to do with being in the present moment. Finding ways to stay in the present will assist you in staying out of fear and anxiety. Finding physical balance with exercise like qigong and walks in the park put you in sync with your "now." Ever wonder why the prescribing of anxiety medication is on the rise in America, with over 40 million persons taking some kind of drug to relieve anxiety, representing 8–10 percent of all prescriptions filled?

Sometimes fear is based on resentment or judgment. It can be indignation or ill will felt as a result of a real or imagined grievance. Resentment is trickier than dealing with non-forgiveness because it carries with it an element of entitlement that presumes your position is somehow deserving or righteous.

Resentment is a perversion of humility, as it acts out as a sense of humbleness that is seated in a false power base rather than true humility. When clearing resentment seek to understand "the little you" who is stuck in self-righteous anger, and validate the self. Choose *not* the anger. Only then will resentment dissipate. Seek then to understand your feeling of entitlement. Seek to understand your feelings of being entitled about a situation or person. Give the other person credit for doing the best they can. Remember that for those who are given much, much is expected. It is never an even playing field. Knowing better expects better, without resentment.

Moving into victimhood is also a perversion of humility as it presumes the innocence of oneself and guilt of the perpetrator. But in reality the situation is never completely one-sided. Even those who had no hand in the affront may have created this as an opportunity (at inner levels) for reasons unknown to either party.

Consider the following example of a client working in the Akashic Records. A woman who had been sexually abused by her father asked her Record Keepers (in session with me as the guide), "What did I do to deserve the abuse from my father?" The Record Keepers stated, "You are a very high being. You chose to stop the madness, and came into this family to stop the abuse." Her response was telling. "Oh my goodness, I actually did. When my father went after my younger siblings, I always stood in the way, offering myself, rather than see them get hurt!" she exclaimed. Remember, it is your judgment of a situation that fuels you to ultimately define yourself as a "victim" or not. In this case, the woman truly was a volunteer of the highest order. She was such a highly evolved soul she knew she would be able to overcome this horrible abuse and heal to emerge unscathed.

WHAT IF YOU COULD CONTROL YOUR RESPONSE?

Emotions can get out of control because they can cause a person to self-reflect on the *emotion,* rather than the present, while re-creating the experience. This can create a circular pattern of anxiety, thereby perpetuating and escalating it! Everything in the universe is moving and shifting. Everything in the universe wants to evolve, including emotion! It is alive with your loosh!* If you fail to direct it, it will follow the path of least resistance. The "programming" to deal with anxiety through medication is only one solution. There are others.

What if you could use the power within you to control your emotions? Emotions can seemingly perpetuate themselves because humans are the royal creator of emotions! This is part of the grand spark imbued in humans as cocreators. You can learn to cocreate with your emotions, but first you must learn to notice and modify the emotions that play into your weaknesses so that you *can* be the cocreators you were meant to be.

There are agendas from beings that benefit from your fear and worry. Knowing that there is a benefit to beings whose agenda runs counter to your own is helpful to improve your determination. There is reason to be concerned and I recommend you revisit that discussion as well by accessing the blog post noted below.†

WHAT ARE EMOTIONS AND HOW DO THEY WORK?

Emotion is the fuel of creation, energy in motion. Emotions are qualified chi (chi that you have infused with a purpose), which allow you to

***Loosh* is a term invented by Robert Monroe, author and founder of the Monroe Institute for research on consciousness, to describe a huge emotional infusion of your light energy into your body. It literally is fear but for humans it includes the "God spark." There is a physical manifestation of negative loosh addiction, adrenochrome, which has been a huge problem for humanity, and has been written about elsewhere. We will discuss loosh in more detail in chapter 5.

†For a detailed discussion of this topic, please see the blog post at https://maureenstgermain.com/your-fear-and-worry-create-negative-loosh-2.

expand and to experience more. Emotions are a driving force in manifestation. Emotions allow you to reflect and reexperience events that are both pleasing and painful. Creating from positive emotions is a well-known technique in manifestation. In the manifestation method of the Genie system, found in my book *Be a Genie,* emotional energy is one of three important elements used to manifest. (The other two have to do with real-time conversation and visualization.)

Emotions take universal high "God energy," or chi, and fill it with a purpose. Chi is unlimited universal energy that is located everywhere. We know that biofeedback can be used as a tool to transform your body's autonomic responses and respond to your commands. I created the 5D Mind Mastery meditation, which includes brain wave entrainment, along with autogenic training to help you teach your body to respond to your commands. Autogenic training is a well-documented scientific tool, in use for over half a century. My 5D Mind Mastery meditation is similar to the one created by Dr. Norm Shealy, neurosurgeon and founder of the American Holistic Medical Association, but with the addition of binaural beats, a type of brain wave entrainment.

Mastering your emotions may be easier than you think and using your emotions to help you fulfill your mission propels you into your fifth-dimensional self.

CREATING WITH HIGH EMOTION— SADNESS OR JOY

Your joyful emotions can expand and fuel your manifestations based on joy. Your sad emotions create fractures in the energy fields that you create, albeit unawares. By doing this, you then create a "wall" to sustain and maintain the fractured part rather than heal it! Holistic chiropractic physician Brad Nelson and his work with the emotion code clearly identifies this connection. The qualified chi (emotion) then is squandered, creating a "false" sense of safety. For sure, emotions are meant to be expressed and released, not contained and used to build walls!

Emotions can also create vortexes in the time and space matrix. These portals, or vortexes, can be accessed by connecting two of the three possible intersections. The three intersections are time, place, and past connection. If you have ever visited a place where there was great travail and hurt, it can trigger experiences from your past or past lives tapping into the energy trapped in that location. A simple explanation of this might be that you were there in another time. Your presence in a location where you experienced big trauma (in this or a past life) will allow you to tunnel into that time of the same place. You can use your connections to a difficult time, in your past or a past life, to heal that past trauma. More importantly, remember that emotions are the energy of expressions (powered-up purpose) that you can use however you see fit. Some kinds of emotions are easier to understand because of their deep roots.

WHAT IS REALLY GOING ON?

I see this energy of human expression to have a certain progression. It starts as an implosion—or going within. This is where reorganization and reinvention occur. As we'll see below, the process of cell mitosis easily reflects this process, first going within after the burst of outer manifestation. This going within allows you to burst forth with your own recognition of who you are and the self-discovery of your full potential after your inward journey.

Let me explain this process of cell mitosis. Think of conception, and the burst of creations. Next the cell division of the birth process follows. *When* the egg and sperm merge at conception, that's you bursting forth into manifestation. *Then* the cells divide from this original cell, producing first two then four then eight cells. Corresponding to sacred geometry, two become four in a tetrahedral shape, then eight forms into the star tetrahedron. *But* when we reach a certain size at the next division—sixteen cells—cell division moves inward. At sixteen cells the outer sphere is formed along with the central core, which later becomes all the internal organs. In all cases the first expression is outward. The outward expansion occurs until the inner expansion takes over to integrate all that has been learned and discovered.

Humanity is transforming into fifth-dimensional beings, along with a fifth-dimensional Earth, as a shared experience. Gaia is ready and waiting for critical mass to occur. Remember, you will not transform everything overnight. Remember too that we humans generally follow a sine wave in terms of our evolution, moving from ideal expressions to the old familiar ones, and then back to an even higher ideal expression. As explained in the book *Waking Up in 5D*, it's like being teenagers. When they finally express wisdom you are so relieved, until they do something stupid. And then they step up even higher. Humanity and life are evolving and shifting through change similarly.

Even though you've heard it before, it bears repeating. You are not your earthly body. You are a cosmic being, a butterfly going through chrysalis. Who knows what you will be when you finally emerge from your cocoon!

2

Curiosity and Joy

Let curiosity bring joy into your life. When you have true curiosity, you have joy. When you have curiosity, you are not in judgment. When something happens that you do not understand, are you quick to label it? Or do you wonder what's going on? Give yourself the gift of practicing wonder, true curiosity.

ACHIEVING YOUR HIGHEST AIM

Ask yourself what your highest priority (of things to accomplish) is right now. I'm going to teach you how to achieve it or resolve it. You'll have to work with me on this and you'll want to do more than just read this book for entertainment (although that will also work, since I'll be sharing a good part of my story along the way).

Do you know what your life mission is? I know mine. I didn't always know. I wanted to be of service to others, and I wanted to make a difference. If you are still reading this, it might be the same for you.

In 1994 I was traveling with a group of people on a familiarization tour. This is a trip where you look at a hotel property with the idea of convincing your group to choose that hotel for a convention. It's common in the tourism industry for meeting planners and travel agents to take these "fam" trips. I was a nonprofit administrator whose mandate was to host a substantial annual meeting that often took place at this type of resort.

I was invited to go on a fam trip—that's a manifestation story I'll share later. But *first* I want you to know that this need to know my mission was literally uppermost on my mind at that time in my life. I was the proud mom of four sons in their teens, down to the youngest who was eleven. My twenty-five-year marriage had ended a year earlier, and I was working at a new job that I loved. The invitation to go someplace nice like Acapulco was highly inviting, especially since the price was right (free)!

One evening on the trip, the activity included dinner and then an excursion to a local nightclub for some dancing. Suddenly I didn't feel well at dinner, but still really wanted to go to the club to dance the Macarena (it was a thing back then). Hoping to feel better, I excused myself from dinner with the promise to return in time to go to the club if I improved.

My host told me later, "When you left the room, it's as if the 'lights' went out. You hold so much joy and light, that we all had a good time while you were there. Yet once you left, dinner seemed flat." In that moment, I realized that I had been given a huge gift. This was the answer to my seeking! I was to bring joy to others—with my curiosity about them, with my wisdom, wit, and light!

As the years passed, I held my mission in my heart no matter where I was or who I was with. Wherever I went, if I felt out of place or didn't know anyone, I made it my mission to reach out and be curious. I realized my curiosity could be contagious. I could light up the room with my love, my smile, my friendly questions, and my joy. I realized quickly that people hungered for what I was serving, and that I could "do my mission" anywhere. I realized that my desire to serve was being honed into a skill to show each person I met that they were *lovable!*

Along the way I wasn't always perfect. I did my best as a mom and learned that being a mom called for some pretty quick thinking! When my supersmart, bored, third son failed Algebra II for the third time in summer school, and after fall classes had begun, I asked him if he was in the programming class he wanted to be in. "Yes," was his response. I said, "Well, that means the paperwork hasn't caught up with you yet. But it will. You will get called into the guidance office and they will tell you that you have to drop that class because you've not qualified for it."

He had missed one day the last week of summer school, and they had apparently drilled into the students' heads that if they missed a day, they shouldn't bother coming back! When I realized that he hadn't gone the second day of the last week after attending four-hour classes for five weeks, I was quite alarmed, but he just shrugged his shoulders. I knew he could handle the subject matter but he didn't do the homework and that's why he kept failing. I asked him, "Now that you've been in the programming class for a few days, how are you doing in it, and does the teacher like you?" He responded, "The teacher loves me, and it's going great!"

I instructed him further on how to handle what would come next. "Well, when you get called into the guidance office, the guidance officer will explain to you that you don't qualify for the computer programming class because you didn't earn the prerequisite." I continued, "You nod innocently and ask, "Okay, if I can get the programming teacher to sign a waiver to let me in, will you allow me to be in the class?" The guidance officer will agree to this because he cannot imagine anyone failing Algebra II three times could possibly get any kind of exception from the programming teacher.

Continuing my (guided) instruction, I said, "Then take this information to your programing teacher, asking him to write a waiver for you." My son reported to me afterward that the programming teacher said to him, "Are you kidding? You are the best student I've ever had. There's no way you are *not* going to be in my class!"

So what are you good at that you don't feel qualified for? What "certificate" or training do you lack that you wish you had? What do others tell you you're good at? What are you waiting for? Many people say that the reason Dolores Cannon, the world-renowned past-life regressionist, hypnotherapist, and author of nineteen books on metaphysical subjects, was so successful at her skill of hypnosis is because she lacked a lot of education—and her lack of professional training actually made her more curious and open to the huge body of knowledge that came through her focused efforts.

In that same era I complained to my sister about a well-known author who I loved and followed, and who had produced an audio-guided meditation that was very difficult to listen to. Her voice was scratchy and even though the content was wonderful, I was only able to listen to it once. In my complaint to my sister I said, "I could do better than that!" and my dear sister said, "What's stopping you?" I can now ask you, dear reader, what's stopping you from reaching for your dreams? So now it's my turn to invite you! I ask you, "What's stopping you from being who you are meant to be?" Maybe you don't think you have a job that is important, but consider this. Even if your job is caregiver in your family, if you are the one who always pulls the family together, you can start mentoring one of the nieces or nephews to take your place, and to help you. Yours is an important job. Family is the backbone of society, and you make a difference in your family and community. You may be thinking that every human knows this—but sometimes we don't remember or recognize that value of caregiver!

Maybe you are the one who inspires others with a book study group. Maybe you'd like to lead a study group, but don't know how to get started. The easy way is to start a book study club at the local bookstore or library. Volunteer your services until you are ready to teach a wider audience. When I moved to a new community and didn't have any "like-minded friends," I started a book study group and met and made friends with people who were with me long after the study group ended.

I recently went to a class reunion. I met with many classmates who I had lost touch with over the years. A few of my closer high school friends took time to look me up and look into what I'm doing now. As my friend who invited me to the reunion said, "Maureen, I don't think anyone in our class will understand what you do."

When one of the guys, trying to be inclusive, talked about "sharing their beliefs, ideas, and tolerance," I smiled and said, "I don't share anything about what I believe, unless they pay me." We both laughed and he realized I wouldn't be preaching to him or anyone else, and that I was there to enjoy the friendship, and bring light into the room by honoring who they were. It was fun to remember their accomplishments, help them to feel loved and important, and help them know they were lovable.

SHOW THAT YOU CARE

What if you approached every interaction with the idea that it was your job to learn about the other person and to help them feel important? How powerful would that be? I don't think anyone asked me about my books, or what they were about. One person did ask the name of one of my books and wrote it down. Nancy, my friend, did buy it, but said it was "really deep," and that she hadn't finished it! I just laughed! I'm so happy she bought it! And I know that someone in her world *will* read it.

Another one of my closest friends from high school who was at that reunion (a lawyer) told me he mentioned it at a dinner party and was shocked that his friends "knew all about that kind of stuff." Remember, I promised to tell you how I manifested my trip to Acapulco in the first place? My first book, *Be a Genie,* details how to use sacred geometry, quantum physics, and new material to manifest things in your life. I called the system "the genie system."

As I was formulating the material for this book, I consciously chose to test what I was getting from Source. Early on in my explorations of the genie system, I decided to use it to win a contest. The objective was to name a new meeting room (function room) for the Princess Hotel chain. This public meeting room was being constructed at the Southampton Princess Hotel in Bermuda. The new construction was a state-of-the-art facility specifically designed for the many medical meetings that would be held there.

The contest was open to members of the association community. My position as CEO of a national professional association made me eligible. A free trip to the hotel was the grand prize. I utilized the techniques I would later write about in my book *Be a Genie.* My visual was of me on the beach in front of a beautiful ocean. I used a picture I cut out of a magazine. It featured a woman in a beach chair looking out at the ocean. I imagined that the hotel behind me was wonderful, and their function room was named the name I had given it. Meditating on it daily at first, the perfect name soon popped into my head, which I then submitted for the contest.

When the winner was announced I was so surprised—it wasn't me!

I couldn't believe it. I *knew* my name was the winner. There must be some mistake! I decided not to be upset and forgot about it. I figured there were lots of reasons why they might have chosen a different winner, since the selected name was pretty ordinary.

About a year later I was invited on a familiarization tour to Acapulco. The travel agent I was working with told me I had to cover the one hundred dollars in taxes, but otherwise the entire trip was free. We would be staying at a first-class hotel. I knew this company well enough to know their offer was legitimate and decided to go on the trip without looking at any of the details.

Upon arriving at the hotel some months later with the group, I was pleasantly surprised. It was the Acapulco Princess, part of the Princess Hotel chain. When I entered my room there was a beautiful brochure on the bed showing their brand-new meeting room. *Wow,* I thought, *this is just like the function room they built last year in Bermuda. They must have used the same architectural blueprint.*

I wondered what they had named it. You guessed it. It was the name I had submitted, the one that "didn't win" the naming contest for the Southampton Princess! Here I was, soon to be sitting on the beach, in the hotel that had a meeting room with the name I had submitted for the identical room in Bermuda. And I was a guest of hotel management! I had received my prize.

Coincidence? Hardly. I had my proof. Here was another manifestation confirming the efficacy of the genie system. There's more hidden in this story. I held no anger or judgment at the "mistake" of not using my name for the contest conference room. I simply let it go. To learn more about the genie system, check out my book *Be a Genie.*

3

Learning Big Secrets

Have you ever wondered what consciousness really is? How is it that we are conscious of ourselves yet believe the animal kingdom is not conscious of *itself?* In the animal kingdom we know that there is some innate ability for pets to find their masters, or animals to return to certain areas they have originated from.

Certainly they don't communicate their awareness of consciousness to us. Yet we know from observing the phenomenon of animals returning to a former home and other associated behaviors that there must be some force within that produces their ability to "find" their owners or the migratory homes they travel to. Surely there is some form of consciousness in the animal kingdom, as well as mankind, even if we do not yet understand it.

WHAT IS CONSCIOUSNESS?

Your consciousness is immutable, present, and observable. One proof of your innate consciousness is your inability to commit suicide by holding your breath. The minute you lose consciousness, your autonomic systems take over and breathing resumes.

I recently opened the Akashic Records to ask, "What is consciousness?" and this is the answer I got.

> Consciousness is awareness that moves through human thought. It is the remarkable ability to achieve awareness with or without a body. Consciousness is self-awareness in either limitless or limiting form. Consciousness seeks to validate itself. Consciousness knows experience through awareness. Some help can be found by stating what consciousness is *not*. It is not thought. It is not thinking, nor is it emotion or emoting. Consciousness is life itself, appearing in all living things to a greater or lesser degree.

To me, the debate about consciousness is a circular one. It becomes a self-referencing statement because it takes consciousness to recognize itself. It takes consciousness to think about what consciousness might be. Yet clearly consciousness is life itself.

Initially, the ability of each of us to identify consciousness is limited by the five senses and our normal responses to normal stimulation. What about stimulation outside the normal realms? What about various forms of meditation? I have read that expanded states achieved by the use of certain drugs also provide expanded awareness beyond the normal physical scope.

Once a person's consciousness is expanded beyond their own physical, observable senses, they have difficulty describing these experiences because their *experience* is beyond their awareness at the *physical* level. Thus we can conclude that consciousness can expand a person's experiences, and his experience of himself. How far can it expand? The answer lies in the beholder.

When we meditate we open ourselves to expanded consciousness and start to experience more "consciousness" than is humanly experienced in nonmeditative states. Humanity has wandered around the mind of God throughout the ages. Proof of this very idea comes from the mystical traditions and teachings of the Egyptians, the Chinese, and the Hindus, as well as the Edgar Cayce material held at the Association for Research and Enlightenment in Virginia Beach. This massive research library preserves the entire database of Edgar Cayce's 14,307 documented readings as well as hundreds of books written about the use of the information found in those readings.

Consciousness in man expands as he uses his mind to unearth his true spiritual nature. Consciousness is the Source! I believe we choose to be human as we choose to expand consciousness. As we incorporate the discoveries of the scientists of the last century (Max Planck and others) into the discussion, we begin to understand that if matter doesn't really exist (according to physicists) then only our thoughts exist. And if our thoughts are a product of our consciousness, everything is consciousness! So consciousness is life itself—it is God, and God is consciousness.

THE IMPORTANCE OF CLEARING

Many people do not realize that there are so many attempts to get humanity to fail, and the overlays and toxins sent humanity's way are staggering. This is why it is so important to know how to clear yourself and to get help when the situation calls for it. I have mentioned clearing in my other books, so we will not go into it deeply here, but it is important to know about.

It's all a game, of course, but the intent to watch humanity fail is serious and can be addressed in a very sweet way.

Clear intention will assist you in finding your way out of darkness. One time when my phones were being bugged (they aren't now, as far as I know) one of my sons overheard me complaining about this and said, "Mom, you're not that important." I remember laughing out loud! I use that phrase whenever I think a situation is trying to intimidate me. I'm just not that important!

One of my very good friends didn't realize her husband was bringing in dark energies . . . he worked at both a bar and a church! Yikes! My first husband and I prayed to Archangel Michael as part of our daily practice. He picked up a side job to help with family expenses, working as a bouncer in a bar after working all day in his day job. He said they never had a single fight in the bar on the nights he worked.

Don't assume that just because you are clear and you're doing your work, that your family and friends are clear. I've seen my current husband inadvertently pick up energies that didn't belong to him on a simple trip to the grocery store! I've cleared him dozens of times, and he lives with me! Think bigger. Think in terms of helping the planet. Lost souls that jump into you are simply doing their part, and you are doing yours by helping your loved ones stay clear. And by clearing them, we are also helping many of the lost souls to find their way home to Source. *Clearing* is the word we use to define the clearing of one's energy fields. (These are the four lower bodies of humans: physical, mental, emotional, and etheric.) There are many ways to do clearing exercises. You may be familiar with smudging or burning a special kind of wood. These are traditional methods that Native Americans use. I teach a much more powerful method of clearing with a stainless steel knife, which Tibetans taught Madame Blavatsky (and handed down through the ages).

✷ *The Archangel Michael Clearing Exercise*

Here is is one method you may not have experienced. It is taught in my book *Reweaving the Fabric of Your Reality.* I start with a prayer: When you clear the entities, you always state in a commanding voice: "I call in Archangel Michael with his nets of blue lightning to clear away any and all entities, energies, and anything that [I] can clear at this time, and escort them to a place of evolution or dissolution. I further ask the Golden Illumination Elohim to assist [me] in releasing all that is not of the light. Thank you." (Please note that the "I" and "me" in brackets should be replaced with the name of the person you are clearing.)

The *Archangel Michael Clearing* method includes the use of a stainless steel knife that you use to cut the space around your body, the same space that your aura would occupy. Make sure you cut underneath the bottom of your feet, and make sure you are holding on to a chair or table when you do so. (I have found even if you well balanced and flexible, if there are entities present they can cause you to lose your balance.) After you cut around your body, make a sweeping arch from left to right (think of a car's windshield wiper) to announce to the universe that you are done.

You can also clear someone else, given that entities are not allowed to be here on the Earth plane anymore. This is an important distinction from what you may have been taught, for example that actions or ceremonies you do for another are usually done with their permission.

✵ *Exercise to Clear Another*

A way to clear someone else is to start with a completely clean piece of paper, large enough for you to stand on. Write the person's name on the paper, then place it on the floor. Stand two paces in front of the paper. Back up one step then wait until you feel like the energy of the person you are clearing is behind you. Back up one more step, placing both feet on the paper.

Next say the Archangel Michael prayer above, using the person's name instead of your own. Cut around your body the same way you would clear yourself with a knife. Then step off the paper, retracing your original steps. On the first step, pause and make sure you can feel the energy pull apart, like "taffy" pulling apart. Once you feel it "snap" you may then take the second step forward. After you have taken the second step, wait until you feel as if you and the other person's energy are completely separate, which may be described as being "all clear." Make sure you burn or shred the paper with the person's name on it when you are done.

In one case Kim was being called by her sister repeatedly to "Please clear me." The sister worked in a telephone quota environment and needed clearing frequently, after which Kim chose to save the paper. Kim received so many requests that she thought to be efficient, she would save the paper that you stand on and are supposed to shred or burn. She thought it would save time, and she would be ready for the next request. What Kim did not understand is that the clearing was "incomplete" because she saved the paper and had to be repeated often! Kim asked me to check in with my guides to "find out what is going on!" When I discovered she was saving the paper between clearings, Kim realized her mistake.

As far as smudging goes, I don't smudge with sage or palo santo wood as a clearing tool because the stainless steel knife is so much more effective for clearing entities. (Sage and palo santo do have wonderful antibacterial, antifungal, and antiviral properties however.)*

---

*If you decide to do these clearing exercises yourself, I suggest you watch my YouTube video on clearing energies. Here you will find instructions to clear yourself or someone else remotely. In addition, if you wish to use our clearing team, you'll find trained experts in clearing energies. I have worked with all of these people over a period of fifteen to twenty years. They are persons of high integrity—accomplished and reputable.

And finally, there are ways to clear other people remotely as well. They may or may not be aware that you are doing this work. Remote clearing is permissible by cosmic laws as these entities or energies that you are clearing do not belong on this Earth plane and are required to leave. Perhaps you have broken the speed limit while driving. Why do you do this? The answer is "because you can." Typically, you won't lose your license if you get pulled over by the authorities. Similarly, when an entity in someone else is pushing your buttons, using your energy to create problems, you have grounds to ask Archangel Michael to escort the energy out. They are not allowed to be here and you have every right to have them escorted out with Archangel Michael's assistance.

FIVE SECRET RAY CHAKRAS

Many people aren't aware of the five secret ray chakras, which are very powerful tools you may add to your skill set. You may wish to learn how to activate and use them. It is important to understand that these chakras have multiple purposes.

The secret ray chakras are used to project Source energy through you into the energy field around you or toward another. One purpose of these chakras is to project energy outward and activate yourself. Second, you may use these chakras to clear and move energy on others. This can be healing in many ways. These chakras are found in the center of the palms of your hands and on the center of your feet next to your arch. The fifth one is on the left where the spleen is located. The inquiry of these chakras as powerful tools is not commonly understood. People do use their hands to project healing, yet do not realize this energy is coming through these power centers.

These five chakras are often referred to as the location of the wounds of Christ. When you hold a baby in your left arm, you energize that baby from that spleen chakra. Babies who breastfeed also get this energy boost every time they nurse on the left side. You can proactively turn on your secret ray chakras to project energy when you consciously activate them. One way to do this is to gently tap the center of your palms and then project the energy that bursts forth.

The work of the five secret rays is linked to your secret ray chakras. It is a "hidden gift" that is tied to the workings of your secret ray chakras. These gifts allow you to bypass the typical points of testing, bringing in mastery without having earned it! They are literally grace points of light that imbue you with all the love and light of these masters listed below. Invoked regularly, you can use the secret ray chakras to bless, heal, and turn back negative energy. Working with this energy you may find you are more self-effacing and your inner awareness becomes more powerful.

When you walk on the Earth with your bare feet, you and the Earth both benefit. When you connect your energy to the Earth, you activate your Earth star chakra (a few inches below your feet) to the Earth as well as the secret ray chakras of the feet. This allows you to have direct communication with Mother Earth and enables you to start to experience your connection to Mother Earth as well as to all life on Earth.

The secret ray chakras will help you to master and purge the more deeply buried experiences, memories, wounds, and biases that prevent you from expressing your true divinity. When you do outer work with your seven chakras, you are processing in the center (of each chakra), receiving (energy and information from others), and focusing on bringing information in a receptive way. When you work with the secret ray chakras, you are working with the unknown (inner) Elohim who are unnamed and who work within the Great Central Sun. Since these energies are secret, not much is known about them other than that you can invoke them and produce a very high energy. The five Dhyani Buddhas of Tibetan Buddhism will help you activate and purge these inner chakras, hastening your mastery.

What can happen when you start to invoke these five secret rays in your daily work? You can expect to be a kinder, softer you. You will notice your interactions have a sweetness you didn't even know was possible. Chanting the names of these five Buddhas will open and allow this energy to purify your inner awareness, your inner thought processes, and outer expressions. I include their names and qualities they evoke: Vairochana clears ignorance; Akshobhya clears hate, and hate creation; Ratnasambhava clears human and intellectual pride; Amitabha clears the passions—cravings, greed, and lust; Amoghasiddhi clears envy and jealousy.

Amoghasiddhi clears your biases, habits, and motives from the mundane human emotions and moves you into higher expressions and higher states of being. It literally magnetizes your fifth-dimensional self to you and anchors more of your divine self into you. When you call upon the Dhyani Buddhas, masters of these rays empower you and assist you in releasing anything that would stand in your way. In this, you anchor a certain portion of divinity within yourself. I have made a chanting recording of this you may purchase on my website.

The secret rays (of the Elohim) are anchored onto the Earth by the Beloved Mighty Cosmos, the magnificent being who holds the entire cosmos in his awareness. These rays carry an incredible energy of balance of the male and female, anchoring in the Divine Masculine in the north pole and the Divine Feminine in the south pole. They are integrated in a focus (etheric retreat) in the Temple of Peace over the Hawaiian Islands. In an effort to understand this, imagine Earth is receiving increasingly higher amounts of this cosmic energy the more you invoke it and anchor it into your own body. Beloved Mighty Cosmos was commissioned by Source to ensoul these secret rays.

✷ *Activating the Chakras*

The way to activate these chakras is by directly connecting to the Tibetan knowledge of the five Dhyani Buddhas. You might say, "I bring in the five secret ray chakras, the five secret ray Elohim, Beloved Mighty Cosmos, and the Maha Chohan to assist me in activating my five secret ray chakras." (The Maha Chohan is the representative of the Holy Spirit, Father Mother God.)

Amoghasiddhi is one of the five tathagata (transcendent Buddhas) in esoteric Buddhism, also known as the five Jinas, and his name translates to "he whose accomplishment is not in vain." Amoghasiddi Buddha's right hand is in the *abahaya* mudra, signifying his fearlessness toward delusion.

Amitabha Buddha's left arm extends downward while the right arm bends upward. Both his hand and face are out, with thumb and index finger touching. This mudra was used to welcome the dead into the Pure Land.

Fig. 3.1. Amoghasiddi is one of the five transcendent Buddhas; he reigns over the heavens of the cardinal directions, specifically the north.

Fig. 3.2 Amitabha is another of the five cosmic Buddhas; he resides in Sukhavati, which is his paradise in the Western Pure Land.

When I invoke the five Dhyani Buddhas, I prefer to announce specifically what I am asking them to clear. I'll name the poison that affects human consciousness and then say their name, with *om* before and after it. Actually, it is ideal to sing it, because it is easier to remember the whole thing that way. This is why I recorded it for you. If you wish to do this right now, you would say: "I wish to clear [name of the poison] with [name of the five Dhyani Buddhas] wisdom." It would go like this.

- I wish to clear the poison of ignorance with Vairochana's (Vair-o-chana's) (ch = like *chocolate*) all-pervading wisdom of the dharmakaya (the great void).
- I wish to clear the poison of anger, hate, and the creation of hate with Akshobaya's mirrorlike wisdom.
- I wish to clear the poison of spiritual, intellectual, and human pride with Ratnasambhava's wisdom of equality.
- I wish to clear the poison of the passions of all cravings, covetousness, greed, and lust with Amitabha's discriminating wisdom.
- I wish to clear the poison of envy and jealousy with Amoghasiddhi's all-accomplishing wisdom, the wisdom of perfected action.

Ideally, you will sing this in any pitch you wish, along with singing *om* before and after their name. In the recording, I announce what they clear, followed by singing *om* and then singing their name. If you do this without the recording, start by singing *om* first, then sing their name, concluding with a sung *om* at the end of each name, and repeat each three times.

Be prepared to be amazed.

One of the members of my Ascension Institute, Mona, was playing my recording at the beach as part of her assignment for that week and a friend was along. The Ascension Institute is a yearlong training program created for more intense study and individual integration with a small group of like-minded souls. Mona had just read the information on the black helicopters in *Beyond the Flower of Life*. Without warning, a black helicopter appeared, came close, then made a right turn and disappeared! Why did I mention the friend? The friend was a witness.

Mona turned to her friend saying that even she would not have believed what she'd seen if her friend had not come along for the beach time and had seen it too.

Remember, the five secret ray chakras are masculine in nature and project the energy of Source wherever you direct it. Keep in mind that the seven chakra system you may already be familiar with is feminine and receptive. It reads the energy of the field around you, and the energy of others. In contrast, the five secret ray chakras are used to send and channel energy outward. Thus, the secret rays channel through the right brain; the seven primary chakras are anchored in the left brain.

QUALITIES OF THE CHAKRAS

MASCULINE	FEMININE
Five Secret Ray Chakras	Seven Chakras
Outward	Inward
Active	Receptive
Straight lines	Curvy lines
Electric	Magnetic

You may use this knowledge when you are working with healing and sending energy. Certain mudras and energies are conducive to certain activation processes. The five secret ray chakras are outwardly activated, projecting energy that you send through those chakras, or that you send from your heart through the chakras. The seven chakras you probably have heard about (base, sacral, solar plexus, heart, throat, third eye, crown) are receptive, and are reading the space/field around you as well as the fields of those you are interacting with. Later in this chapter you will learn a new way to activate your seven chakras.

How Can I Use This in a Practical Way?

Consider that activating the secret ray chakras is done first. You may bring clearing energy to a person or situation to activate your secret ray chakras by calling in the five secret ray Elohim. Then hold your hands in front of you, palms facing each other, a few inches or centimeters away from each other. Create an energy ball (between your hands) of activated chi—chi filled with a purpose—by first pulling a channel of love and light from your heart, which you will fill in front of you like a balloon. You will then ask for the light from the Great Central Sun, the five secret Elohim, and your own masters and guides. The light will adjust the channel when you command "that it be expanded, amplified, and adjusted for the highest and best good" of the person you are sending it to. You will then hold your hands open to hold this energy ball between your hands, waiting until you can feel the energy shift and change. You will be able to feel its completion and then tie it off like a balloon in front of you and send it to the situation or circumstance you have named. If you can, invite the recipient to accept it. You want to tie it off because you've filled it with your unconditional expanding love and do not need to be tied to the other person.

K-17: COSMIC SECRET SERVICE

Many years ago I was given (in meditation) the name of K-17 as a master to invoke to assist in the elevation of human efforts for Divine Government. As a proponent of spiritual mastery for all, I created a guided meditation to help leaders worldwide be their most evolved selves. When you are upset or disappointed (with leaders of any kind) you can do something productive by praying for them. (You can download the Divine Government meditation for free on my website.) Next you can invoke the presence of K-17, who is the Ascended Master who heads up the cosmic secret service on Earth. I have been involved in this training for a very long time.

I was given K-17's name as a resource. There are many individuals (like me) who are doing this work. Years later I found a reference to it in the book *Masters and Their Retreats* by Elizabeth Clare Prophet. Up until then I thought I was getting supersecret information. In a way I guess I was! In addition, I was also given the information on a ring-past-not. This is a tool used to limit and seal energy, or an area, with an energetic, impenetrable tubular wall.

Later I found that same information in Prophet's book. It started when I began to use the cloak of invisibility, which I invoked for the purpose of moving about without being noticed. This has been helpful in many ways when being called to be in places that some might call dangerous. For sure one would not invoke the cloak of invisibility without understanding its effect and true purpose. Furthermore, one never leaves it in place, and always asks for it to be removed after any special activity is completed.

Don't do this at home: One of my students was driving her car up the West Side Highway in Manhattan with another student on their way to my class one evening. She had picked him up on the way. They had decided to invoke the cloak of invisibility around them and the car so they wouldn't get pulled over for speeding! What they had not counted on was other cars pulling out in front of them and a few near collisions! Each of them asked their Higher Self what was going on. What did their Higher Self's tell them? The cloak of invisibility had made them invisible to all the other drivers! They made note of this and reported their story in class!

You can call in a "ring-pass-not" to create a tube of white fire around a situation, building, or person to prevent something from entering. You simply name the situation or location within the statement: "I call in a 'ring-pass-not' around [the name of person] for the purpose of [name the purpose]."

4

The Magnanimous Dimension

So what is it really like being fifth dimensional? I listened to Dr. David E. Martin, a brilliant businessman, economist, and philosopher, speak about the social distancing of 2020, and at the end of the interview he talked about love. He stated that it is not love when we allow someone with a "title" in our lives—be it mother, father, or other socially important person—to insist their beliefs must be ours too. How do we deal with the injunction "Honor thy father and mother" from the Ten Commandments? You allow them their truth and you stand in your sovereignty.

The following story, told by a very spiritual client and friend, illustrates this point. She is someone who is usually in her fifth-dimensional expression. She writes: "This is the 5D experience. I thought you might be able to use it in your work when describing how 5D can open here in everyday events":

> Last Friday night I attended a local arts council event in town. The energy was high and I could hear and see truth everywhere very easily. Several times I was guided by my guides to say something to someone that would be helpful to them. It was stuff I had no way of knowing anything about except that I was seeing truth really easily with my guides' assistance.

The energy in the room was increasing when an aunt of mine came in the front door. I said hello to her and she acted like she was going to hug me. Then, as I responded with a motion to hug her back, she pulled away and pointed her finger at me in a scolding manner. She announced that I had not been to visit her in a very long time, and that she was mad for that. This also had the insinuation that I was to dutifully visit her soon.

Without thinking at all I saw the truth of the situation and—with a *big* and *powerful open heart* and not one speck of guilt arising anywhere—I said, "I am probably not ever going to visit you," and I hugged her. My heart was so open and I spoke the truth with such gusto and absolute profundity that even though she knew she should have been offended, she and the seven or eight people witnessing this were flabbergasted and amazed. All of them couldn't help but smile. I could see them looking for somewhere to put this in their brains and then they just gave up and joined in on the huge field of *heart* and *truth* that all of us had just created. They all smiled.

Later I realize what had happened. This was an old pattern where people (especially older Southern relatives) used guilt to control others. It would appear that we all came together to be the antidote to that old pattern of manipulation and control. I thought to myself "I don't do that guilt thingy" because *the option of responding with guilt had not even occurred to me.* This made me think of the man on the subway trying to take your money (Maureen's story from *Be a Genie.*) When you said, "I don't do that," he found it so confusing that he simply gave up. You can't argue with the truth!

MOVING INTO THE FIFTH DIMENSION

How do you move from a lower dimension to the fifth dimension? When you consciously do the exercises I've offered in this chapter (and in other places too, such as in chapter 2 of *Beyond the Flower of Life*), you will find that you are easily sliding into and staying in the fifth dimension. All the tools I've taught you, along with the many tools I've told you about, will help you step into your power. Remember, in

Waking Up in 5D, I explained why you might choose to stop saying, "I have to . . . ," because this statement gives your power up to whomever will take it. The effort you make will assist you in completely lining up your emotional body with your physical body. This in turn will allow you to slip through the fourth dimension with such momentum so as to move through this "nexus" upward into the fifth dimension. Remember that the fourth dimension is the zone of high emotion (joy or sadness, for example), but it's also a portal to get to the next dimension. And remember, you can slide between the dimensions. That's why the Nine called the three dimensions (the third, fourth, and fifth) "the Magnanimous Dimension." Claim that and coexist in all of it.

When your emotions are balanced, they align and move quickly through the fourth dimension and into your fifth-dimensional body. This is when you may easily align with your highest purpose and your most evolved self. Remember, the wormhole exists like the path to a combination lock: all the places line up and match and you slip effortlessly through to the higher dimensions.

You can accomplish this shift in several ways. The easiest way is to start with a clear intention and then work things out from there. Begin with a visual or an intention that clearly shows the results of being fifth dimensional in a third-dimensional body. Your first objective is to make sure you are lined up. How do you do that?

Notice what resistance you have in your body. Notice what resistance you have in your mind. Notice your resistance in your heart. Invite all of this resistance to be released. Sometimes it's released through movement (somatics is ideal), sometimes it's released through exercise (qigong is spectacular for that), and sometimes it can be released through various outside healers and other therapies. For instance, one may use resonating and balancing stones or essential oils. I have helped to create tools for this such as the Vibranz Intention disk and the AroMandalas-Orion Oil Blend Series. Your willingness to utilize tools like this will make light work of it.

Ask yourself now, "Am I in resistance about anything? What can I do, or use, to help me open up to higher expressions of me?"

This book will help you mine and tap into your own inner database. The body collects nonlinear information and this book will help you begin to interpret and understand this information. You are already collecting this "intuitive" data through your seven receptive chakras.

Another example of living in the fifth dimension (which is nonlinear) is illustrated in the example of a young couple trying to purchase a house in a very competitive market. They did their inner work and when they found the house they wanted, they knew there were several offers on the table. They asked their realtor to include their heartfelt letter, which explained why this house would be perfect for them and the children they hoped to raise there. Even though they were not the highest bidder, the sellers were so touched by their sincere offer that they chose to sell to the young couple!

LINEAR INFORMATION

We are beginning to grasp what it means to be fifth dimensional, and as we have learned, I equate it to being nonlinear. Yet, what do I mean by linear and nonlinear information? The linear example is based on the idea that there are two inputs of data that occur to produce a result in reality. Technically this is not entirely true, as everything is codependent upon everything else. However, we will use scientific terms here to help you grasp the concept of linear versus nonlinear. For example, a linear equation that almost everyone understands is distance equals velocity times time. This is expressed as the equation: $D = V \times T$.

Most people don't realize that they are actually using a formula that is known as Newton's second law of motion. It's a simple mathematical problem to figure out that at thirty mph, one will take two hours to cover sixty miles. However, although this is a simple formula, it doesn't consider other factors such as traffic and so on. Anyone who drives knows how to use this formula. There is a direct relationship formula, meaning that when you change the numbers on one side of the equation there is a direct proportional change of the numbers of the other side of the equation. If you double the speed, it will only take half the time. This is a linear equation because each part of the equation has a direct relationship to the other parts. When you increase or double the speed then you cut the time in half because there's a direct proportion.

On the other hand, nonlinear information presents the idea that "if, then." In truth, if something happens it presumes that the next "then" will happen. In most cases (and in the scientific method) we use the ability to repeat an experience (or experiment) over and over to create a sense of knowing that if we do that same thing again we will get the same result.

What if you could do the same thing you've always done, yet get a different result? Of course, some have called this insanity. However, it is also known in quantum physics that a researcher may set out to measure a particle, that's what shows up, this is what they are able to measure. Simply by changing his intention a researcher can receive completely contrary results to what he expected. It is a proven scientific fact that in the measuring of a particle or a wave of the electron photon we find that the researcher's intentions about what to measure are what show up to be measured.

CHAOS THEORY

Chaos theory can be explained using the analogy of a game of pick-up sticks, or that of a rolling snowball that creates an avalanche. Factors go into the system without any apparent change in the system. We now know from science that everything's far more nonlinear (chaotic) than we had ever imagined. I'll poke fun at a commonly used phrase by a mother, "Put your coat on, it's cold outside. You'll catch cold." The child calls back, "No I won't!" We all know it's true that a person can go outside in the cold and not *catch* a cold. Even if it is common to get sick or ill from being outside in subzero weather, it isn't *always* true.

This then means that we too can create an outcome that is possible. It may not be the most common probability, but it can be a possibility. If you jump off a cliff, you will not fly. Being human, you cannot manifest wings on your back. However, there are things that you can manifest simply by thinking them through. The concept is to use your mind and in so doing, consider possibilities that you would like to see manifested, whether or not they fit into the "probabilities" category. Being in a linear mode is a way to organize thought but it limits what you might expect. Logic in any direction is still linear. When you take up too much polarity (left to right, top to bottom), you keep the polarity game engaged. Seek not to understand but to imagine. Remember, polarity exists because it gave us what we wanted. Now that we know we can choose differently, we can end the game, exiting until there are no more players.

Original humans were multidimensional beings who could manage multiple awareness and multiple time lines. Humans could take "the road less traveled" and the traveled one as well! Imagine being able to watch multiple shows on a TV. It is called "picture in a picture," or PIP. This is a TV you can own now. This helps you begin to appreciate multiple realities simultaneously. You don't have to be locked in 3D all the time. We are anchoring in awareness of what it's like to be fifth dimensional. First you notice the similarities, then the differences.

A man in my class was using a Hemi-Sync CD (left brain–right brain synergy training) in his meditation. He was driving down the highway when he suddenly had an image of a gold SUV in his mind's eye. He slammed on the brakes. Then a gold SUV appeared, pulling out right in front of him and cutting him off. His early braking prevented a collision.

Another man tells of a story where he starts his day with a "prayer of protection." He begins his story by telling me, "The car next to me was totaled. It was a big pileup and the original car that went out of control actually landed just inches away from me." He says, "I *knew* that it was a cosmic event."

LORDS OF LIGHT

We are the Lords of Light* working with you this day. We wish to inform you your carriage that you are taking to your next *now* being upgraded. We want you to see yourself in a beautiful horse and

*The Lords of Light are a conglomerate of high beings who have moved into the Earth plane to assist the transformation of humanity.

buggy carriage, imagine a royal carriage that has beautiful gilding on the outside and a beautiful design, padded seats that are luxurious, and beautiful springs on it. It is so lovely! Like the one that Cinderella's pumpkin turned into. And we also wish to say to you, you may remember your old carriage being like a wagon of the Wild West. And now you are in this beautiful carriage—so your vehicle that you are taking has now been upgraded.

Now we've deliberately used the cart image—for those of you who perhaps do not have an affinity for automobiles—to help you understand that you are still being *towed*. Maureen used to say a joke. When people asked her, 'How do you know where to go?' the response was, 'I go where I'm towed.' And everyone would laugh because it's a play on the American word *told."*

You are being towed to an expression in the reality that not only feels luxurious, and allows you to feel well provided for. So you have an environment of no worries, an environment of comfort, an environment of enthusiasm. You are now traveling in a golden environment. We ask you to do the meditation that is on Maureen St. Germain's website called the Golden Time,* which will reinforce this.

We want you to breathe a sigh of relief—Ahhhh. We want you to look around yourself and decide, What can I create?

We want you to pretend that you are an extraordinarily well-off individual who will choose what you want based on what you like, not what you need. You are not afraid to let go of things that you have liked in the past because you know you can get more. And the new will be just as pleasing as the old even though it will be new and different. The reason we bring this up is because we want you to begin to be less attached to what you have—attached for fear of losing—and instead move into a level of security that pleases you.

One year at Christmas Maureen told her sons, "When you pick up a Christmas ornament to put on the tree make sure you really like

*This meditation is available for readers to download for free at www.MaureenStGermain.com/5DSelfBonus.

it. And if you don't really, really like it, you can put it in a box over here that is going to Goodwill, a charity organization." Well, there were more ornaments in the Goodwill box than there were on the tree, and yet the tree looked absolutely fabulous! We want you to feel like that—to know that if you got rid of half of your belongings you would be okay. You would look upon that and be very content.

We also want you to notice the people in your world who have resources. Perhaps they have an inheritance that they're living on, or they have a big company that they own or work at, and they choose a very simple lifestyle. They recognize that the more belongings they have, the more work it is to maintain those belongings. So we would like to encourage you to understand that you could expand your energy by decreasing your belongings. This will allow you to devote more time and energy to your spiritual growth and to your spiritual mastery.

The road you are on is filled with love and light. The discovery of who you really are will amaze you, as you have never thought of yourself in these terms as a cocreator. Keep in mind that the world is changing. The world that is coming in front of you is the result of your prayers, of your requests, or it's a release from the drama that you have experienced. Initially, it will feel like a magical world. So we ask you to keep your eyes open and your heart open. We ask you to look at life with wonder and joy. We invite you to explore what you can create, now that you have begun to understand that *you* have far more mastery than you thought. We ask you, as you read this, to tune to your heart, and turn to your heart.

Tuning to your heart is you *sensing* the vibe in your heart. Turning to your heart is moving your *mind to be heart based.* This is a dance where you are using your emotions first to tune to your heart, then you use your mind to put your intention on your heart. Then we ask you to see it expand and grow. We ask you to feel the love that we hold for you. We ask you to be filled with appreciation and gratitude for this beautiful world you live in—for everything that you do have. We ask you to stay in a place of deep gratitude for everything that happens to you.

If you encounter something that you find unpleasant, we ask you to ask yourself, I wonder what good am I going to get from this experience? We ask you to hold your tongue and not complain. Perhaps you will complain to one close confidant who is more like a sponge or a dry towel and who will listen to your tears, but you won't need to correct them and you won't need to repeat your story. And this way you confine your disappointment in life to a minimal amount. This is very important because you are being *towed* to a much greater place than you have ever thought possible.

Right now keeping your heart open and your attention on your heart is your most important action. Do not let anything dissuade you from this. You are a magnificent being. You deserve the very best and you are getting it. So sit back and relax and enjoy the ride. We are the Lords of Light.

THE LORDS OF LIGHT

A NEW NORMAL

Maybe as humanity becomes fifth dimensional, it is recovering lost tools and lost codes that will permit it to break through these so-called barriers of linear time. As you begin to understand that timelessness or simultaneous time is the norm in the universe, then you will be free to use this awareness to get even more out of life. Then you will have the time, time codes, and multidimensionality to expand your experiences and heal yourselves and the planet.

Everyday fifth-dimensional experiences are now part of your new normal. This means you will see and experience things that you had never imagined possible. You will "walk through walls" and be able to avoid accidents and difficulties by being in fifth dimension. But how does one get there and stay there? We will get to that—but first we want to whet your appetite for experiences that have been reported by my students and friends.

How many experiences have you had that you knew beyond a shadow of a doubt that it was not normal in third dimension? One of my Ascension Institute members was worried about a friend who was in the hospital. She prayed for her, sent her heart energy to assist her, and then checked in with her Higher Self to see if the friend was going to be okay. Her Higher Self signaled "yes," it would all be okay, yet she still had concern and wondered. Then she set out on her errands for the day, and while driving past a random hospital she saw a very clear image. In the sky above the hospital was an angel! For her, that was a wonderful confirmation that everything would be all right.

HOLDING THE FIFTH-DIMENSIONAL VIBRATION

It's easy to slide out of the fifth dimension if you don't take care of yourself. You want to eat the best way for you, and you want to get plenty of rest and plenty of water. Are you still using third-dimension energy and playthings to serve yourself, such as illicit drugs, or too much food or gossip? Feeling tired or run down may be a signal that you're using the 3D version (thinking, judging) to activate your emotions, using up your energy instead of healing it.

Do your best to focus your energy on things that make you feel good—joyful experiences and positive thoughts. Do you best to claim your right to be in the fifth dimension. Hold your energy close and don't let yourself fall into gossip or drama. What anyone else or everyone else is doing is not your game.

Every time you do not get what you want, remind yourself, "This, or something better." That will help you validate and hold your fifth-dimensional vibration. Allow all your stories to flow naturally. Bless them, don't fight, don't pay attention to the little stuff you don't like, just remind yourself "it all turned out well." Notice the use of past tense is a purposeful creating of the future. This is especially important when you have no idea how that will happen!

Remember, Sanat Kumara said, "The game is over. It will end when there are no more players. Will you be the first to leave, or the last?" Knowing this allows you to choose where you wish to stand. Remember, it's all a game, and the game is over. You can unhook from the game anytime you wish. Remember your staying in judgment about anything puts you back in the game. The game will end when there are no more players. Unhooking from the polarity of judging yourself or others is your exit strategy, to help end the game.

You can only be a victim once. After that you are replaying the experience, milking it for sympathy or validation. The universe wants you to have what you want . . . but it needs you to name it. When you cannot think of what you want to name it, simply announce to yourself that you are really, really happy! Remember you are Source; you are part of the greatness of all. And start validating your 5D experiences.

Here's another example of being in 5D. I received this note from one of my students in San Diego. She writes:

> This story involves my husband. I came home one day before my husband did and parked my car in the garage. I started making dinner. I heard him coming home, parking his car in the garage. He came in and was surprised that I was home. The first thing he said was, "Where's your car?" I said, "It's in the garage." He said, "No, I did not see your car!" I said, "How could you not see my car?" I said, "Okay, let's go see." We both went to the garage. Voila, my car was parked next to his! I said, "Do you see my car now?" He was so surprised to see my car. Interesting that he had to walk by my car to get into the house and there was no way he could miss it. He must've been in 5D, a really good place, and didn't see it! *Her husband was in 5D coming through the garage (and the car didn't exist in 5D).*

In another instance, a friend, Marbeth, returning late in the evening, put her favorite family heirloom ruby ring in a drawer one night after wearing it. She didn't want to lose it, so she tucked it in the dresser drawer for safekeeping because she was tired. The following morning she went to retrieve it, and it was not there! Every time she looked for it, to put it away properly, it wasn't there. After three months, she finally gave up, and announced to herself, that "It must be lost," and made her peace with the loss. The next time she opened the drawer, there it was right on top! Why did it happen this way?

YOUR ENERGY DICTATES YOUR VIBRATION

Your vibration is a match for the fifth dimension when you are at peace, when you are joyous. When you are worried or anxious that you might have lost something, you are in a state of polarity—I don't want to lose it, I must find it—that is a match for the third or fourth dimension. Third and fourth dimension have polarity, so fear and worry would be a negative polarity. Keep in mind that there is nothing wrong with this, just like there is nothing wrong with being in third grade in school, unless you are a capable fifth grader! Even judging yourself will knock you back into the third dimension. This is why you get to be mellow, like a grandmother who loves her grandchildren but doesn't need to parent them!

How do we live in life but not judge it? Well this is where it gets interesting. You strive, you reach, and then step back. You work hard, you sign up to get things done. If you miss the mark, you try again, without too much fanfare. Think of how many would-be lawyers take the bar more than once. It's okay, it happens. You go on.

In a sweet TV interview with the late Dr. David Hawking,* Oprah Winfrey asked him, "How do we advance our perception vs. (the actual) essence civilization?" I believe she was asking a deep question about the future and people's true essence of their humanity. His thoughtful reply was, "Humanity will develop the discipline to act with constant and universal forgiveness and gentleness without exception."

Consider this: As far back as the fourth century BCE, we find this quote: "Every man pursues only the good; only his perception of good is always changing. Mankind's consciousness is going be passionate for God, not for belief systems, and allow for your ascending levels of consciousness!"†

---

*Dr. David Hawking (February 28, 1913–February 24, 2002) of the famous *Power vs. Force* book, was a professor whose interests included the philosophy of science, mathematics, economics, childhood science education, and ethics. He also served as an administrative assistant at the Manhattan Project's Los Alamos Laboratory, and later as one of its official historians.

†Socrates was a Greek philosopher from Athens who is credited as one of the founders of Western philosophy, and as being the first moral philosopher of the Western ethical tradition of thought.

How does our growth occur? Slowly at first, then explosively, corresponding to the principles of sacred geometry.

DECEMBER 5, 2016
EL MORYA AND THE LORDS OF LIGHT

We are the Lords of Light helping the Earth and her inhabitants transform into their new reality. Be aware and be prepared to let go of anything and everything in a case where you may be required to do so. This does not mean that disaster is imminent. What it does mean is that you're so willing to shift and change that you could be willing to let go of your past wounds, your past hurts, and your past disappointments. By choosing to let go of those consciously, you greatly enhance your abilities to come away from this transformation with the garment of light that is so pleasing to you. You will not care that you have left baggage behind. If you were to go on big trip somewhere, and when you arrive you are told your suitcase has been lost, you could be upset and you could mourn the loss of your favorite shoes, your favorite clothing, or your favorite jewelry. Or, you could say, "Now I get to go shopping! Now I get to try new things. I get to create a new wardrobe."

El Morya and the Lords of Light

When you are fifth dimensional, even a lost suitcase doesn't seem to be a problem. On one three-week trip to China, my suitcase arrived on my last day there! Auspiciously, during the previous trip I had ordered a dress to be made for me, and it wasn't ready by the time of my departure. My organizer had picked it up, and it was waiting for me when I arrived on my following trip. No one minded that I taught for three weeks in the same dress, least of all me. At least I didn't have to teach in my travel clothes!

I know of a family who lost everything in a house fire on Christmas Day. The creosote in the chimney caught fire from the Christmas wrapping paper the father was burning in their fireplace. The roof caught fire and it was all over in minutes. One minute they had everything and the next minute the house had burned to the ground. They barely got out with their lives. Do not put yourself in that situation. Cancel that thought. Simply observe that and say "Oh, I can choose to let go of anything and everything right now." "And let it be painless. Let it be pleasing, let it be inspiring, let it be encouraging. Let it be exciting that I am okay with letting go of my old ways of acting, and my old ways of believing, and my old place of experiencing life in my interactions with others. And I welcome my new opportunity to be one of the many who are totally connected and plugged into one another and Mother Earth. I'm choosing to be part of the new reality that many have already connected to." In this way you will make your transition to the new fifth-dimensional you—to your new self—with grace and ease. You may not have to let go of your treasures and the things that you appreciate.

Let me cite the story of a channel who had an incredible experience of loss in her life when five friends canceled a Sacred Journey simultaneously, which caused financial ruin to stare her in the face. She went to bed that night and said to the Ascended Master El Morya, "I think I am bankrupt, but I have my health. I can always start over if I need to and *if there is a solution I must know it by tomorrow morning.*" Indeed, El Morya provided her the solution by the next morning.

EL MORYA AND THE LORDS OF LIGHT

In this way, you'll start to shift. Ask for my help and I will provide it. This channel was optimistic about the future in spite of her profound impending loss. Let go with grace and ease so that you are not suffering by hanging on. Your suffering will be minimal.

We are at the place in time and space where suffering is no longer a *desired experience.* Nor is it *required.* Many of your belief systems have taught you that suffering is a way to purify who you are. And it is not. That may have been true in the past, but is not true at this time. Temper your responses. Temper your worry and fear with joy, with gratitude, and let the universe surprise you with the amazing opportunity behind that. If someone you love wounds you, this is a typical disappointment on the planet. There are energies that would prefer you stay wounded because they are being *fed* by your energy. When you reinvest your own energy in these feelings, you're actually *feeding* the energy that wants to perpetuate this feeling. This becomes the addiction to the emotional drama and pain. We recommend you go into the space in your mind and tell yourself, "I do not wish to give free rent to this issue in my mind. I can choose to let go."

You might say, however, "I don't want to (let go) because I don't feel validated. So let me take a moment and ask my angels and guides to show me how important I am. Show me how much I am loved." And as a practice, especially during this time of emotional drama, you might say, "Dear God, show me how much I am loved!"

Asking your angels and guides to show you how much you are loved means that your choices can unhook you from your drama. Does it take away your validation? No! Choose to let the angels validate you instead. They know who you are and they love you! This is an aspect of yourself that you choose to give less attention to.

The second thing is, every time you go into that drama (with your thought), with your pain and suffering, remember to ask yourself the question, "Did I get anything from this? Did I get any benefit from this painful experience?"

Perhaps there was a benefit at some point. Maybe you learned something by the experience, maybe you had good times, maybe you traveled to wonderful places and have happy memories too. Even though the connection is now nonexistent, you can put your attention to lots of good memories. When you carry old memories, choose to go right into your powerful, joyful ones. Train yourself to follow your sour thoughts with the sweetness of the benefits of the experiences, the learning, the opportunity, the happy times—and let that be the last taste in your mouth. In this way you will shift your mental body and expand your heart and emotional body. We bless you for reading this. We create for you, a matrix of love and light that reading this will create in you. When you are so stuck that you cannot take any of these actions, you can simply call upon me, El Morya, by saying, "Help me step into my divine matrix. Help me step into my divine plan." And I will step in and make your way straight and you will know that is so. You will know this is where you need to be. And you will succeed by calling me in. And I will say, "I will not disappoint you when you call me and *you* will not disappoint *you* either." Thank you and good day. I am El Morya with the Beings of Light who have stepped in to give you guidance as you move into your awareness for the coming year.

El Morya and the Lords of Light

5

The Great Forgetting and Using Fear to Fuel Your Ascension Work

As you approach your memories, you are going to be facing many opportunities to "right the wrongs." You can decide, as you review experiences, that it doesn't matter, and your memories will soften. If you use your mind to let your opinion be amplified by your emotional reaction and judgment that someone or something is to be punished, you will stay in the third dimension. You can, instead, decide that *you* are now in charge of your reality and that *you* alone can change your own personal reaction. *You* can change the matrix of how you experienced an event or events.

As an exercise I am going to ask you to focus on one event, but you will be able to do this with anything that troubles you. This is because memory is *not* stacked sequentially, but is *event* related. Any "near event" that bridges the space-time continuum allows you to see and feel and experience the first, or former event. When you realize that certain locations and situations will trigger past painful memories, you can choose to heal them when they emerge for "reconciliation," and then you will be able to merge these time lines into your memories.

MERGING TIME LINES

Remembering past traumas begins a certain way. There are node points in time and space that allow you to access information (tunnel down) that you have either forgotten or been blank-slated (to not remember). A node point is a point on a time line that is parallel or close to another time line. The node point can allow for them to merge permanently or partially. You may have a trigger occur, which is usually in that same physical location, with or without a similar situation, and the mind is able to tunnel back to the original event. This is significant.

Using your understanding of node points, you may clear out old wounds by revisiting a past wound and then remaking it into a new version of the past. Imagine you are the director of "your movie" of pain and suffering. It's done with a simple meditation. You can literally sit down quietly and make up a new version of the painful story. Then allow it to be real in your mind's eye. This will allow you to create the solution to your issue without a lot of other effort. First take a moment before you start and playfully imagine the same situation with a new and more pleasing outcome.

Humanity is about to forget about all the pain and suffering we have been through. We are merging multiple time lines and this is part of the great forgetting. The merging of time lines is part of a greater action to heal and transform experiences. Humanity has suffered over its suffering. Man's inhumanity to man has caused huge suffering that is now not tolerated nor likely to be created again. This inhumanity was the result of certain forces influencing humans to choose darkness over light. That era has ended and will not be revisited. Humans have used memory to revisit their pain and suffering. They did it to ensure they would not do it again. Unfortunately, there were those (dark forces) who thrived on negative loosh.

THE WEAPON USED AGAINST HUMANITY

We are at a stage in our spiritual evolution where we are clearing out our old baggage so that we can squeeze through that wormhole that is the fifth dimension and beyond. You may have heard the biblical phrase: *squeeze through the eye of a needle.* It's a similar thing to what is being described here. We are merging the many versions of ourselves into one—to move into higher dimensions.

If you are tricked into believing that you are *not* capable of doing something, you will act as if you cannot! There is a matrix in place to support the lie, and the liars depend on this lie to control the masses. If you weaken their matrix, then you weaken their ability to hold you hostage, to use this lie as a weapon against good men and women.

You may use the information contained here to help heal the mind and spirit of humanity. In this, you restore humanity to its highest level because in your heart you know they were lied to, and that something was terribly wrong, even though you might not be able to pinpoint it!

The new powerful woman is strong—yet not aggressive. She has mental strength yet has a gentle touch. Her wisdom leads, as she allows others around her to do it "their way." No overpowering to convince. Many women were trained in the masculine methods to be powerful yet are finding their own authentic feminine voice of leadership. When you do what someone else wants, because they force you, it may make you angry. But when you stay in your power you are able to stay clear and soft, yet persistent.

The perversions of the Divine Feminine are still being eradicated. Many have been pulled into or tricked into performing the worst acts, the most horrific acts against sometimes even their own children! In one such case, a true story of my client, his wife was born from an act of debauchery perpetrated on the family to hold them in silence. The child took on the mother's shame. This child grew up and was not able to swallow. As an adult she was so "choked" up that she had to have her epiglottis (swallowing organ) removed so that she could still eat. She still cannot speak her own truth. There is a deep family secret that the family will not name, even though some of them know of the truth of it.

There was a story in William Tompkins's book *Selected by Extraterrestrials* about how the head of a military department of secret programs would require various team members to host Friday night dinners where the department head would ravish the host's wife in front of everyone for all to see, and then be sworn to secrecy on all matters lest their shame be revealed. The product of one such union, now a woman herself, took on this wound so the mother could heal. She was loved, but conceived illegitimately, to hold a secret.

All of humanity has been lied to, and we are now exposing those lies. Let us not choke, but let us find our way out of the dilemma. Why would the lie of Mary Magdalene be perpetuated? Why would Mother Mary's firstborn daughter be a problem? The world was not ready for a female leader. Everyone was expecting a male heir and the secret was kept to protect her, and to regroup.

Negative loosh is a fuel source for the energies that would have you fail. Loosh, being life-force energy (chi imbued with a purpose), can be either elevating or lowering. *Loosh* in this usage describes a negative experiential syndrome. As we established earlier but bears repeating here, loosh from painful and difficult circumstances was a desired fuel (for not-God energies) since it contains both the God spark and the human creative spark. It's a picnic near an anthill. Wonder who you were feeding? Some call these beings "the powers that *were,*" with emphasis on the *past* since it is now on the wane. Even calling them by name will give them power, so I do not mention them specifically.

On the other side of this, the planet is being bathed in uplifting loosh, coming from sources of love and light, helping us transform. This positive loosh is irresistible and joyful! This is the energy found in so many uplifting experiences, deep meditation, beautiful gardens and architecture, playing with a pet or baby.

Make no mistake, this hologram called the third dimension does have both positive and negative loosh. Our goal is to pay attention to our joyful, happy moments, and laugh and optimize them, remaining balanced at every turn. You can recycle and evolve your sad, unresolved emotions by practicing two-fers and more.

WHAT ARE TWO-FERS?

While I was in college I asked my angels to help me out of a difficult depression. They advised me that I was to name two positives for every negative thought. I did this consistently in thought and speech. Within one week of transferring into a new college, the director of admissions was asking me to lead tours.

I remember my mom saying, "Talk about the blind leading the blind!" I share this story with you to make a point. Even the direst of circumstances can have a silver lining if you look for it. The universe continues to give you more of what you put your attention to. Barbara L. Fredrickson, Ph.D., a pioneer in the study of positivity, has studied and written extensively on this subject. Ongoing scientific study of this phenomenon (positive thoughts to replace negative ones), sometimes called the Losada ratio (3:1), established that three positives completely eliminate any negativity and reframe reality significantly. It is also true that as long as the positivity outnumbers* your negative thoughts (by 2:1) you will shift and change!

When you discover you are remembering or reexperiencing a difficult time, every sad or painful memory is a thought that pulls you down. What if you could train yourself to recognize these thoughts as contrary to your evolution? You can do this by training your self-reflection to notice your inner critic and by asking your angels and guides to alert you when you have a negative thought. Create the new habit that every time your attention is drawn to the negative, you'll follow it with two or more positives—to transmute and transform that energy ourselves, rather than waiting for our emotions to be harvested and used as fuel by forces that do not support our evolution.

You've heard the phrase *birds of a feather flock together*. Well, your thoughts are like that too! Thoughts are little bits of energy or "chi-bits" that collect and merge into bigger "chi-bits" or thought clouds. Like attracts like. You are throwing bread crumbs (just like in the tale

*A 2013 study conducted by Nicholas J. L. Brown, Alan D. Sokal, and Harris L. Friedman challenged the validity of the Losada ratio. Their concerns stemmed from an empirical viewpoint. They did not find issue with the idea that positive emotion is more likely to build resilience or that a higher positivity ratio is more beneficial than a lower one. They found issue in assigning applications of mathematics to pinpoint the "ideal" emotional ratio (Brown, et al., 2013. *Complex Dynamics of Wishful Thinking: The Critical Positivity Ratio*).

of Hansel and Gretel), which will build pathways in your brain that will follow the same path.

Unresolved chi-bits will float away from you and find other chi-bits like themselves and merge with them, growing in size! They are loaded with your emotion. In fact, emotion is what colors chi—or gives chi its purpose. When we imbue our thoughts with a purpose we are infusing emotion into the chi we have garnered. When we fail to express, resolve or recycle our emotion—eventually it floats away.

FOLLOW THE FLOW

When humanity was created, humans were given the ability to cocreate with God by infusing chi with a purpose, creating what is now known as emotion. Chi, or raw energy, exists everywhere in unlimited supply and is readily available for you to garner and imbue with your beliefs and desires. You do this almost constantly. The practice of qigong actively harnesses and directs this energy for your benefit.

By filling chi with a purpose (e-motion), you create energy that is distinctly different from free-flowing energy or chi. Creating emotion moves chi from being two-dimensional and flat into three-dimensional consciousness and aliveness in the third-dimensional reality.

Creating e-motion (energy in motion) is what humans do best. This "giving energy a purpose" is one of the *privileges* and distinctions of being in a 3D body. Saturating chi with beliefs and desires that contain the God spark adds intensity, direction, and fuel to all of your events or relationships.

SURPRISE OF THE SYSTEM

It was anticipated by Source that emotion could cause pain and suffering so it was instilled with a certain limitation: it must be expressed. Initially this was meant to ensure there wasn't an overflow from one event to the next. In other words, emotion was meant to be used up in each moment of the creation of it, the fuel for true resolution.

ALL EMOTION MUST BE EXPRESSED

This means that once you create emotion from your own beliefs and desires, the next step is to allow their *expression so they can be resolved.* Understanding this flow will help you begin to grasp how important it is to not only express but to *resolve* your emotions as well. At some point, instead of resolving our unexpressed emotions, we developed all kinds of other ways of dealing with them. We pushed them into the body—we buried them in the emotional body or the mental body or worse. All of this makes humanity sick. Humans are still discovering thousands of ways we have done this—and now we are *undoing* it. We had pushed it into memory—and used "replay" to create *more* hurts and wounds.

PLAYING WITH FIRE

Humans began to hide these unresolved emotions instead of resolving them. If you don't resolve your pains, they will grow while you are not looking. Everything in the universe is moving and shifting. This is why when your self-talk matches what an outside critic is saying, you can overreact! Everything in the universe wants to evolve, including emotion. It's alive with your loosh!

Your emotion is like fire. Fire is very useful. We use it for so many things in our modern life. But if we start a fire and fail to put it out, it will grow. Very few fires die out on their own especially when they have a ready supply of fuel. Since you know there is plenty of chi to supply your emotional trauma and drama, can you see how you could be feeding alligators unwittingly?

WHAT IF YOU DON'T LET IT GO? WHAT IF YOU CANNOT LET IT GO?

This is where the trouble begins. The action of resolution validates you. It completes the circuit of creation/resolution. If you are not accustomed to self-validation, this will not feel like "enough." This is when you begin to replay your wounds, creating a downward spiral that's harder and harder to extricate yourself from.

Additionally, you attract entities and energies that "feed" off your unresolved emotions, your loosh. (Remember, it is chi imbued with your "God spark" purpose!) This can pull you into fourth-dimensional vortex-type energy, dragging you down, creating an energetic cyclone, sucking the loosh that literally feeds the fire of hurt emotion. But then what happens?

RESOLVE OR RECYCLE YOUR EMOTIONS

Honor your experience of an event and let it go. This means express your anger, disappointment, rage, or whatever and then let it go. If you cannot, then move to recycle! If you must repeat it, limit your expression to only three times. Keep track. If you keep reviewing your emotion, you are simply replaying it and refueling it, not resolving it. If you manage to suppress it, it can come out in illness and hopefully you will at least deal with it then! Emotions can rule you, or you can rule your emotions by cutting off the fuel. You can bounce around for a while or you can take a leap and get out of the drama.

THE WATERCOOLER EFFECT

Humans gather in the office around the watercooler, the coffee shop, or the bar to share their experiences. Somewhere the habit of comparing "bad" experiences started. "You think that's bad, you should hear my story!" Use it as a trigger to walk away. Step away from those situations and groups—no words are necessary. Choose, in each moment of discovering your unresolved emotions, to recycle or resolve them.

Here's your metaphor: I was the support person for a friend who was about to have surgery. I had been through of this kind of surgery with one of my sons and knew these kinds of repairs on the body could be painful. The anesthesiologist reassured me, saying that the anesthesia also had drugs in it that would make my friend forget. Twenty years ago, upon hearing that, I was horrified! I thought the doctor making such a decision was out of integrity. He assured me this was commonly done. I still could not wrap my brain around this. Their agenda was to help the patient heal, and having them forget the pain and suffering would help them heal faster, they thought.

I was concerned about the rights of my friend to make that decision. I now understand that our thoughts can lead us toward happiness or away from happiness. I wasn't so sure these drugs should be administered without the patient knowing in advance, but don't take my word for it. Ask any friend who's been under anesthesia if they remember much of what they went through. One friend actually told me all her memories are messed up since her last surgery.

Why is this important? We will all begin to be more aware of duality, allowing it or walking away from it. We will remember choices we have made, or that family and friends have made. And then we will seek a better choice, realizing later that the "old way" in which one used to react or think is another time line that we are choosing to abandon. That abandoning will lead to forgetting. The forgetting will allow the wisdom to remain and release the trauma. This is why the great forgetting is so important.

One year, while working on the manifestation book *Be a Genie* I had "sequestered myself" in my home during the winter upon returning from Egypt (i.e., I bought food for three weeks, with no intention of leaving the house). But I started to get sick the third week. Knowing that I hadn't "caught" anything since I'd not been out of the house in over eighteen days, I asked my Higher Self what I should do. My Higher Self told me to take oscillococcinum! This is the homeopathic remedy used for the flu. I knew I hadn't been exposed to the flu because I had been housebound for three weeks.

I always follow my Higher Self, so I took the remedy as directed. The next day as I described my symptoms to a friend over the phone, she said, "It sounds like you have the terrible flu that is going around." Since I didn't have the TV or the radio on at all the entire time, I didn't know anything about it. I asked in meditation what was going on. It was explained by my Higher Self that I did have the flu that was going around, and the energy of the flu involved more than just "catching it from someone" as one would traditionally believe. This was back in 1999, before I had moved to New York!

6

Amplifying More Power Centers

Many ancient cultures *knew* that a clear third eye was related to a functioning pineal gland. The pineal gland is very small, perhaps the size of a grain of rice (five to eight millimeters). The third-eye chakra and the crown chakra are two chakras that lead into it, forming a right angle between them as they do so. This right angle is important as it allows for a shifting to higher dimensions. Remember the story earlier where my client was listening to the singing of the Dhyani Buddhas, and the helicopter came in, made a right turn, and disappeared? It's not the singing that brought attention to her, it was *her* singing, and the activation of her power center that allowed *her* to shift dimensions. Do I think that the helicopter that she saw was a real helicopter? I do not. I've seen other recognizable things in the sky that are cloaked ET flying devices. What if she broke through the dimensions in such a powerful way that these "outsiders" were checking her out?

Keeping these two power centers (pineal and third-eye chakra) clear means greater connection to Source, more mental clarity, and higher states of meditation. Research tells us that electromagnetic radiation, EMF, is harmful to the pineal gland. Add to that, every public place you go to has overlapping Wi-Fi signals, smart meters, and networks using the radio waves. If you are living in an apartment, you may have this barrage of overlapping Wi-Fi signals constantly from your neighbors!

Many grocery stores are crisscrossed with overlapping Wi-Fi signals. It's hard to imagine, but I've been in grocery stores where every part of me was in piercing nerve pain. When this happened I thought to myself, *I have to find some place to go sit down!* I didn't think it was the location. I thought there was something going on within me, but the minute I stepped a few feet away from the store, the pain was gone! Instantly. Asking my favorite question of my Higher Self, "What's going on?" I was immediately shown the Wi-Fi energies, and reminded of something I'd read a while ago about grocery stores using Wi-Fi electronics to track inventory. If you are sensitive, you may have felt this energy, not realizing what it was. If you must shop in a store with this kind of energy, staying as far away as possible from the center of the store is the safest. When you go into the middle aisle, move quickly!

THE PINEAL GLAND

The pineal gland is very sensitive to variations in light. Sleeping with a mask or towel over your eyes is almost as necessary as sleep itself if you intend to advance your spiritual work. Do not settle for a "little bit of light." Controlled light exposure is the key. It's controlled if you allow light while you are *not* resting, and then enjoy complete darkness while you *are* resting. Even if you need to get up in the middle of the night—to check on the baby or anything else—cover your eyes when you are back in bed. You will find you will rest better with your eyes covered, where even the light from a small night-light isn't visible.

Circadian rhythms are the natural cycles of the body. The pineal gland works with them and relies on the infusion of light to regulate the body. As at home, you will get a much better rest on a plane, or even during a catnap, if you cover your eyes. Complete rest requires that your body has complete darkness. Also consider running your computer, tablet, and phone on night mode, to help reduce the overabundance of blue light that can affect your pineal gland, cause eye strain, and more. Even though too much blue light can be harmful, blue colors can be helpful!

Perhaps surprisingly, the greatest amount of damage to your pineal gland can occur from fluoridated water. This is hard to avoid,

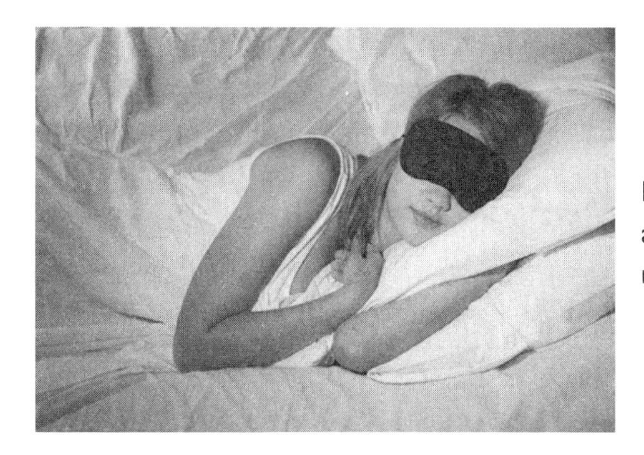

Fig. 6.1. Block out all ambient light for a great night's sleep.

because even some bottled water has been fluoridated. The way to know is to check the company's website and find out their practices! Fluoride is also found in many dental and medical products. In addition to toothpaste, it's often found in bonding agents and even restoration materials. Many foods can harm or damage the pineal gland and unless your food is organic, you may not know what chemicals or toxic substances are in them.

PROTECTING THE PINEAL GLAND

When you are potentially exposed to fluoride always do something to clear it out of your system as quickly as you can. Rinse thoroughly when the dentist gives you the chance, and don't swallow! Exposure to fluoride is pervasive. Even if one's drinking water is not fluoridated, salt, and even milk often are. Fluoride is used in food packaging, so the odds of never handling fluoridated items or of never having been exposed to it are quite slim. Fluoride is quite poisonous. Even at one part per million, it is toxic. It causes fluorosis and calcification, especially of the pineal gland but also other parts of the body. It is nearly impossible to avoid, which means you might want to take steps to keep cleaning and clearing your pineal gland. Tamarind can help you clean out your pineal.

What can help the pineal gland expand and activate? Foods can heal. Food including raw chocolate, cacao nibs, organic kelp (for the iodine content), and goji berries are some of the more well-known foods people take to support their pineal gland. Inversion exercises (headstands, shoulder stands, and inversion tables) are also fabulous, for they flood blood to the head and the pineal gland, which allows it to be bathed in nourishing fluids. It's also great for getting a good night's rest to spend a few minutes in your inversion position before bed. As well, if you're having a sleepless night it helps to get up and invert for a few moments—and then go back to sleep effortlessly! It may be helpful to buy an inversion chair for doing your inversions unless you are innately limber and athletic.

Another thing that's highly beneficial to the pineal gland is getting outside in nature. If you can, go into a park that doesn't have Wi-Fi, without your cell phone. This will help your body calibrate to the Earth. Wear leather-soled shoes or no shoes when you can, as that will improve your connection to the Earth through the secret chakras covered in chapter 3.

Another wonderful way to improve the functioning of your pineal gland is the little-recognized sound frequencies called solfeggios. Certain frequencies are *known* to improve the pineal gland's functions, including music that resonates at 938 Hz. There is plenty of healing music available for the discriminating listener. My favorite is by Kev Thomson and it's called Solfeggio Frequencies 2013. He does have other recordings but this earlier one of his is a favorite of mine.

More ways to improve your pineal gland include the use of blue colors and blue stones or crystals. For example, lapis lazuli, blue topaz, and blue calcite all help to open and clear the pineal gland. In the category of aromatherapy, you'll find that a bath of wonderful aromatic patchouli will take you into a deep meditation. Finally, I wish to remind you of the AroMandalas-Orion Series Blends that work to help you improve your connection to your higher centers. One of the ideal ones for that is Inner Guru. I also use Covenant and Convergence for work of a higher level.

ACTIVATING THROUGH THE HIGHER FREQUENCIES OF COVELLITE

There are a few very specialized crystals that I have been drawn to for the purposes of expanding my connection to Source. You may recall that I featured a number of them in the book *Opening the Akashic Records.* My favorite of all time, for the purposes of channeling, is the quartz crystal faden. I recently was at a trade show and my attention was drawn to the covellite display of one of the vendors. It called to me, and I immediately bought some of it for members of the Ascension Institute.

We used it on the third eye and pineal gland in meditation. Your pineal gland regulates your experience of time. It is important to note that as a stone of transformation, it will help you clear out negativity, replacing it with linkages to positive aspects of your past, your past lives, and your potential lives. It can also open pathways for you to hear and see into higher realms through out-of-body experiences and lucid dreams. As an aside, it is also the number one healing stone to use for cancer. You may look up this stone in the many crystal books that are available.

I created the covellite meditation to help you to find your way through this. This instruction had not been released to anyone except in the private Ascension Institute groups. In the process, one of the very talented members of this program had some amazing experiences that I am sharing here. It's important to know that these experiences are already in the reality, and that following these instructions will allow you to follow the path that has been created by others. It is much easier for you to find your way on the same path that someone else has already created. This is important mastery work that you can do on your own. This meditation is also wonderful for manifestation. So after you have done the activation steps, you may repeat the meditation when you are wanting to manifest something.

To do this meditation you will need two covellite stones of any size and a faden quartz crystal. For the covellite, I like to use one rough stone and one smooth stone. Covellite is rare and expensive, so you can write the word *covellite* on two pieces of paper to substitute for the actual stones. When you do this, make sure you are clear in your intention to access the actual energy of covellite. For the faden you may use a similar technique of writing the name on a piece of paper, but I think you will find many uses for faden, so it may be beneficial to purchase a faden stone.

Start by doing the covellite meditation with your faden on your heart and your covellite on the third-eye and crown chakras. You may use a pillow to get it to stay where you place it. It will start to move love and light through you. You may feel the energy in your perineum, where you will pull it upward toward your heart to raise your chi to your heart. Your heart will "qualify this chi" for your highest and best good, and then fuel the activation of your third eye and pineal gland. This is important because you are opening the gateways to higher consciousness.

You may find this exhilarating. You may find the energy surge affects you in the same way a physical orgasm might, but in the energetic realm. The goal is not to produce an orgasm but to amplify your chi so it may be used as rocket fuel to your connection to Source. One student writes, "The whole process is creating an increasingly powerful and joy-filled vortex inside these connected rays of light. I feel like Superman, with all this love and light moving through me."

When you place the crystals (stones) on the crown, third eye, and heart, experiment a little with the placement until you find the "ideal" spot. It will "click in" or stop moving and then you will know you've found the ideal location for you.

The ultimate goal is to produce an antenna-like effect (in you) that will allow you to tap into your fifth-dimensional awareness and beyond, at will. At the same time, you step into a place of universal service to consciousness by activating in this way. You will only need to do this once.

Phase two is after you have completed the full activation of your pineal gland through the guided meditation below. You will then be able to anchor the connection more fully into your 3D body. This is an important step because it means that you are consciously becoming fifth dimensional. You will put your two stones, one in your right hand and one in your left hand, over the secret ray chakras. Proceed with the meditation. Once again you will only need to do this once.

I've copied the text of the meditation here, but it is preferable that you download it so you can focus all your attention on the experience.

Covellite Meditation

Understand that this stone carries the capacity to create a blueprint (geometric form) for whatever you are choosing to manifest. Each time you do the meditation for the same manifestation (the item you wish to manifest), you may see the geometric shape become more complex. Your mind may be limited, even if you do not see the matrix that forms, and the blueprint will be clear (in consciousness) with the use of the covellite. Be sure to decide before you start this meditation what you will manifest.

THREE BELLS AND TONING TO START

Imagine this stone is helping you to be grounded to Mother Earth, and all of your chakras are in full agreement with one another (and you have the stone with you). Put it on your third eye. If you don't have your stone with you, pretend you are putting it on your third eye. (You may even use a small piece of paper with the word covellite *on it.) Then put it in the middle of your forehead, which is slightly above your third eye, and send it backward into the middle of your head. Then let it drop into position, making a sharp ninety-degree turn, landing just above your brain stem, where it will merge with your pineal gland. The pineal gland is the key or anchor point of all manifestations and all activations.*

Next, as you hold your stone at the level of the pineal gland, imagine it can easily move into your pineal gland and send the energy of your stone, your covellite, into your pineal gland. If at any time you get tired of holding it, you can put it down. It won't matter; it will be fine.

Your stone will activate your pineal once you have placed it on your forehead. You can also put it on your crown chakra and see it stepping into the place slightly to the back, in the middle of your head, moving into place on the pineal gland.

We now want to invite the covellite to assist in manifesting our dreams. We are picking one dream in particular (for each meditation);

one particular miracle that you are seeking for yourself. Remember, manifestation requires a clear field, not because you need to earn it, but because any dark thoughts could manifest along with it. Be clear.

Now that you can see it as a reality, what's new and different in your world, see the covellite providing you with the matrix. You do not need to know what the matrix looks like, but it will be a three-dimensional geometric structure, much like some of the sacred geometry you have seen. It is going to stay connected to you and to your heart's desire. We ask for this according to God's holy will.

Once we have acquired that thing that we have named in our heart's desire, we know that it will be accompanied with humility, because this stone has the ability to create and to continue to provide humility.

One of the things that you may experience during the actual activation is that your fifth and sixth chakras may feel like there is energy pouring through them, and actually there is. It may feel like a soft but powerful movement (like a soft finger moving around, yet under the skin). When you do the second activation, with the covellite on top of your secret ray chakras, it may feel like you have energy circles racing around in the palms of your hands!

Please also refer back to chapter 3, where you learned about activating your secret ray chakras. Remember, your higher chakras may be used proactively because they are "outer focused." When you walk on the Earth barefoot, or with leather-soled shoes, you interact with the Earth frequencies. This allows you to be the antenna for data transfers. These data transfers are energy transfers that will give you a tune-up, allowing Earth to use your vehicle to anchor in the higher frequencies.

As you step into your true power, you may find yourself having dreamtime experiences like this student reported:

> *I want you to know that, in the last dream I had tonight that I woke up from, I sealed a portal—using the technique I remembered when we were in Egypt in 2010. I think it had to do with sealing an energy of drug abuse on the planet. I saw the portal location*

and initially was afraid, so I didn't do anything. Then when I was no longer afraid, I went back. I called in Archangel Michael and laid down energetic "bricks" to seal the "main entrance" and then literally, confiscated the "keys" to that chamber. Then Archangel Michael energetically destroyed a "lesser" opening—like an explosion, but I could perceive it only with my third eye. I spoke to the people there who once were my friends. I told them I'd decided not to go along with what they were doing—they were perverting spiritual practices they had learned, such as clearing work, using it as a false sense of power for themselves and those they cleared. They were also doing drugs.

7

Forgiveness Is Not Necessary

Verbal Attack in 5D

What do you do when you are attacked verbally? If you are fifth dimensional and someone attacks you, are you just supposed to let them do that and not defend yourself? And the answer is: When you are in 5D you don't notice or hear the terrible things they say. You only hear the love behind it. It is not easy to get this until you are in a place of love but think of a time when you were "in love" with someone new, and you were so happy. No one could offend you; you were so loving and forgiving to everyone around you. A bad driver pulled in front of you, and you made excuses for them by saying, "Oh, they must be having a bad day."

In the first *Matrix* movie there is a scene where Neo is dodging all the incoming fire from weapons. He is bending and darting around so well, you can tell from the look on his face that even he is amazed at his skill! When you are in fifth dimension, the energy of a third-dimensional barb or attack is not in your "range of experience," so you don't feel it or observe it, just as we don't register certain sounds that a dog can hear.

What does this look like? My younger sister died in a car accident. She was the "darling" of the family and everyone adored her. She lived in Paris with her French husband and three daughters. A few weeks after her funeral in Paris, a family gathering was held at another family member's bed-and-breakfast. It had been planned a year in advance by my stepbrother to celebrate the birthdays of his father and his wife's mother, who were both turning seventy around the same time. He and his wife owned a beautiful bed-and-breakfast in Napa Valley and they closed it down for this family event to host family members who would come from afar.

My stepfather had two children, a daughter and a son. His daughter and he both had sharp tongues and didn't know how they hurt people with their comments. I was in a huge state of bliss having done my "grieving" over my sister's death purposefully, canceling all my workshops for three weeks to stay home and work through my pain. I didn't want to "fall apart" teaching a class and I knew it was necessary for me to heal before moving on to my work.

I was in bliss because I was so happy at seeing my family members so soon after this terrible loss. I knew we wouldn't have scheduled to have a family gathering that close to the funeral, except that we had all promised a year earlier that we would meet, albeit to celebrate another occasion.

Henry, my stepfather's son, introduced me to some people I didn't know. He looked at me, referring to me as "Gerry's daughter." Musing out loud he said, "I guess that makes you my stepsister." After he left the room, his sister Nancy arrived. I made the introductions and added, taking Henry's cue, "This is my stepsister Nancy." At this Nancy immediately exploded, saying, "We're too old to be stepsisters! Our parents didn't marry until they were over sixty-five!" I just smiled at her, saying, "I just lost a sister and I'm just so happy to have another one." I was totally sincere and in a truly joyful state. I think now, from my standpoint in the fifth dimension, that I hadn't even realized that she could be offended by the title of stepsister.

Throughout the long weekend she did similar things, calling me "the Ice Queen." To amuse myself I told myself, *Wow, she must know that I was a queen in Egypt in a past life.* At the final dinner she chose to sit at my table instead of next to her husband. I was surprised, to say the least.

At dinner she asked me, "What do you eat?" as if that would give her a clue to my peaceful state. She then inquired if I ever traveled to her city. I admitted that I had a workshop coming up in her home locale in a few months. "When you come, would you come to visit me?" she inquired. I said I would check the schedule and see if there was enough time for me to add days to that trip. I was also "stalling" so I could check in with my Higher Self.

I wondered if going to visit her was a wise decision. I found I could manage the extra time, so I checked in with my Higher Self and received the answer that it was completely neutral. It really wouldn't make any difference one way or the other. I decided to visit her on that trip and she treated me like a queen. At the end of my visit, she thanked me for coming and said, "No one from the family has ever come to see me!" This brings tears to my eyes, when I think of it.

"But all the bad people need to pay for their deeds," you might say! Good can triumph over evil. Putting an end to evil does not require that the evil ones be punished. It means purging that energy from the system so that it can never wreak havoc again! This is because the game is over. "They got away with murder," you say. I agree. They did. But on the other side of all this drama is so much good that we can allow ourselves to look beyond it. Remember, we chose to be in embodiment at this time. We chose to be part of the mayhem and the magic.

BIRTHING A NEW REALITY

Many of you are wondering what could possibly be next. How do we get there from here? The ascended master El Morya once thundered at me, "Just show up!" I was terrified at the moment because I didn't know how I would provide for myself and my growing family with no job, no money in the bank, and lots of bills including a mortgage. I couldn't see my way out of the dilemma!

Our job at this moment is to birth the new reality. Birth isn't easy, but we love the idea of a new baby! Babies are a lot of work, and that is where we are at. Fortunately, we now have the ability to be multidimensional. Wait, you didn't know that? Well, think back on the last few months . . . were you able to be completely in your joy by instilling love in your heart in spite of surprises or challenges? And did things go smoothly when you did so? Yes? This means you are in fifth dimension. Then think of the times you've focused on your disappointments or regrets, or you've "lost it"—that's third dimension. Your goal is to choose to express yourself at your highest frequency, which will put you in complete alignment with the rebirth and the higher frequency of Earth.

Humanity has many ETs of the light, and also Ascended Masters who can support you and help you. You can ask for their help. That is the *one* thing you *can* do—and *should* do. You do not have to do this transformation yourself. Remember, the 3D game is over, and you have a choice. *It is over and will end when there are no more players. Will you be the first to leave or the last?*

Civilization takes time to adapt and adjust. Your job is to be open and receptive to new and exciting opportunities to help solve the world's problems. This is true even though you may think that certain terrible things have happened and that the solutions are nonexistent. Yet for each problem there is a solution. Some have already appeared. For example, there are organizations that are clearing and cleaning the oceans. Another organization is helping underdeveloped countries build water wells to give them basic opportunities for farming and health. This is occurring in spite of all the other outside influences and actions that you may think are moving in the opposite direction.

Earth is ready to transform into a new system of love and light that allows you to be the most evolved you can be. Where will you be in this transformation? If you continue to judge others (and ultimately yourself) you will continue to lock yourself into the third dimension.

In the book *Beyond the Flower of Life* I wrote about the three Earths. I was shown this in the year 2000. One Earth was taking the Ascension route, one was the "do-over Earth," and the third was the "crash and burn" version. The Ascension Earth will be interacting with the "do-over Earth" to assist humanity's highest evolution. Which one will you be on?

THE EMERGENCE OF ASCENSION SYMPTOMS

If you can remember who you really are, a whole new level of love and light may permeate your entire being. While your body is adjusting you may need to pay attention to physical issues. This means your physical body will be different. The changes you will experience will be noticeable to you. You'll feel what lots of people call "Ascension symptoms," which I have detailed below.

For sure you must eliminate any kind of physical, mental, or spiritual discomfort by seeing professional healers, allopathic doctors, and naturopaths among others. Energy healers may be able to determine whether or not you need additional outside assistance. If you are having any of the symptoms listed below, do not let any of them go on for a long period without checking in about them with trained professionals.

The next most important thing is to check in and ask your Higher Self, "Is this mine?" A recent client reported after a difficult emotional situation that he woke up with a "fire in his belly." He assessed his situation, realizing that nothing new to upset him had occurred in the past day or evening, and announced to himself, "This is not mine!" Immediately the fire in his belly was gone. You may have picked up someone else's energy and not even realized it! If that is the case, you may wish to do clearing work on yourself.

Some have used the term *Ascension flu* to describe this; however, the word *flu* attached to the word *ascension* seems inappropriate. Even though the symptoms may remind one of the flu, it seems inappropriately negative terminology so I do not refer to it this way. I consider Ascension symptoms an opportunity for growth as it means our bodies are evolving and transforming into higher consciousness beings. The symptoms all relate to how our body will process the experiences. This is similar to when you first start going to the gym. You may have had sore muscles because you overworked them or used them for the first time. Over time, your Ascension symptoms will abate as you adjust your rest, food, and exercise habits.

Not everyone gets these symptoms. If you do get them, please do not claim bragging rights! In all cases they are because some part of you—body, mind, or spirit—is in resistance, either due to unfamiliarity or due to adjustments that are occurring faster than you can move through them.

Symptoms may last longer than a year—again, see your medical professional for symptoms first and rule out anything that may need attention from them.

Physical Ascension Symptoms

- Sinus discomfort, increased infection of the lungs or sinuses, which actually expands the space for the pineal gland to get larger. However, this enlargement may also be from cleansing the body in general. Please review solutions below.
- Coughing that may be coming from heart chakra clearing
- Body temperature fluctuations
- Ringing in the ears (tinnitus)
- Belching (see more on this below)
- Irregular heartbeat
- Changes in appetite or food preferences (i.e., you're no longer interested in eating meat for no particular reason you can think of)
- Sensitivity to noise and light
- Nausea and dizziness
- Lightheadedness and vertigo
- Fuzziness and dizziness, which may include motion sickness
- Sensitivity to noise and light
- Frequent waking for urination (which may not be a sign of aging, for the bladder might not even be full!). Sometimes this is because you are being worked on in your dreamtime and your "unseen helpers" may create this agitation to get you to shift and move.

Mental Ascension Symptoms

- Seeing apparitions
- Swinging from ecstasy to fog and back
- Vivid dreams
- Heightened sense of clarity
- Short-term memory problems
- Anxiety

- Moodiness or emotional purging
- Reading the minds of others and not knowing it until they tell you
- Increased interest in spiritual matters

Emotional Ascension Symptoms

- Moodiness and mood swings
- Greater sensitivity to your own feelings
- Fatigue or overwhelming emotional exhaustion
- Sensitivity to another's energy and feelings (remember to ask, "Is this mine?")
- Crying over things that you never cried over before
- Laughing uncontrollably without apparent cause or source

Working with these changes makes the body strong and more able to move at a higher vibration. Or if the upgrade is not happening as smoothly as you would like, working with these changes will help to facilitate this.

Solutions

- Don't judge yourself.
- Don't resist; resistance can and will prolong or intensify symptoms
- Meditate more; listen to guided meditations. Particularly useful are the Golden Bowl, MerKaBa (both the classic and the 5D MerKaBa), and the 5D Mind Mastery meditation.
- Spend more time in nature.
- Get more sleep.
- To produce more nitric oxide (the natural virus killer) consider taping your mouth shut at night with a small postage-stamp-size piece of first-aid tape. This will ensure that your mouth stays closed, which will aid in the production of nitric oxide.
- The most common experiences are light sensitivity and noise sensitivity. Do whatever you can to minimize these in your life. Again, cover your eyes comfortably at night.

James Nestor, researcher and author of the book *Breathe,* interviewed hundreds of experts on breathing and the ways that people have improved their breathing. The guided meditation *Golden Bowl* has numerous reports from people stating their sinuses open up with this meditation. Breathing tools are known to improve your meditation. Holding your breath on the exhale (comfortably) is a well-known Tibetan longevity practice. Finally, humming is also known to increase the production of nitric oxide, which greatly improves any sinus condition.

In my research for the Activate your Sixth Sense Golden Bowl* meditation, I discovered that the sinuses, all of them together, front and back, have been called the Golden Bowl by mystics. I found a reference to the Golden Bowl in one of the books of wisdom in both the Hebrew and Christian versions of the Old Testament. It is found in Ecclesiastes 12:6–7, written in the third person by a man examining his life and his experiences.

This verse also refers to the silver cord, which is important because it's my belief that the two are related.

THE SILVER CORD

The silver cord is often referred to in the spiritual literature as the cord that connects the spiritual body with the physical body, especially when you have an out-of-body experience and the cord keeps you tethered to your body so you don't die. It's also known that when the cord is broken, the physical body is laid down, and the spirit body is free to return home to God.

The quote from Ecclesiastes is as follows: "Remember your creator now when you are young before the silver cord of life snaps and the Golden Bowl is broken." In verse 7 it continues with "and the spirit returns to God."

Edgar Cayce spoke of an experience that he had with the angel of death. Cayce also referred to the silver cord connection. He was surprised

*Winner of the COVR Gold 2020 CD of the Year

to see that the angel of death was a beautiful being carrying scissors, certainly unlike many familiar depictions of this being. But note that in Ecclesiastes 12:6–7 the writer encourages us to act now and not wait until we are old and it's too late to do so. As mentioned earlier, the Golden Bowl itself is a group of sinuses. They are in the front of the face and continue all the way to the back of the skull, encircling it. There are actually twelve sinus cavities in the human body and the particular purpose of each of them is not known. When we take this into consideration, together with the biblical quote, we can begin to see that there truly is a spiritual use of the sinuses. The Golden Bowl refers to these air chambers around the nose and face, which, again, extend to the back of the head. These air chambers and small glands are the receptors or the spiritual sense centers that receive one's cosmic connection to Source. Imagine—your sinuses could be your inner satellite dish! This higher intelligence is now able to come through you, with the use of this meditation clearing and activating it, opening you up to receive the communication.

At the fifth dimension there is a continuous flow from the cosmos, thus making you an open channel to Source that will help you clear not only your physical sinuses but will open you up to your mental-body and spiritual-body receptors. The feeling of the sinuses opening is the physical manifestation of the expansion of these receptors. The Golden Bowl meditation is extremely powerful for you to access the hidden aspects of your sixth sense, which has been closed off to you due to all kinds of pollution.

An Elaboration on Belching

As noted above, another strange but valid Ascension symptom is repeated belching, especially after a clearing or a profound ah-ha moment! Initially I saw this frequently in China at the workshops I was teaching there. The students wondered what it could be! Initially I felt it was coming in as some form of clearing. I knew it was usually coming from someone who had self-doubt about the effectiveness of the spiritual work they were doing. At this point the belching would occur. It happened so frequently that I started to congratulate individuals when it happened, as my guides directed I should do. They said clearly that it was a confirmation that these individuals had achieved their intended goal.

One of my Chinese repeat students complained that she was burping very often, many times a day. Before the Akashic Records classes she'd barely belched at all. This was a stellar student who had wonderful answers in class. She was such a natural, giving highly impressive information from her Record Keepers. She wondered why, if belching confirmed her spiritual work! When it didn't happen during the Akashic Records training, she thought she was missing out.

In the book *Opening the Akashic Records* and in my live trainings, I teach about *markers,* which are identifiable physical experiences that show up on the body, like a GPS would, to help you find your way. They help the student to recognize that they indeed are in the Akashic Records. Some of these markers are soundless sound (a form of white noise in the inner awareness but not audible to others), pressure on the chest, indicating the presence of a connection to the Akashic Records. This particular student had also complained that she hadn't received any markers!

The Record Keepers spoke through me to her. This is what they said: "You of all people, do not need markers! Everyone in the class is listening to your answers and wondering why they are not getting the amazing information that you are!"

"Yes, but I don't get any form of confirmation!" she complained.

As detailed below in Vilma's account, I explained to this student that at one time in China, there was a healing sect that used belching as a form of confirmation of their work! That version of herself came forward to "confirm to her" that she was indeed getting good information, to validate her self-doubt! I asked her whether or not when she went to her favorite store if she then needed a GPS to return home. She smiled and said, "Oh, now I understand!"

If you have encountered this issue and you do not want to be belching all the time, go into a meditation where you meet up with the version of you who used that form of confirmation, thanking them for showing up in your world at this time and helping you to recognize and accept that you are accurately bringing in divine information. Then ask Archangel Michael to escort that version of you home to God. I was asked to review author and radio show host Jean Adrienne's latest book, *Conjuntio,* on this subject, and here's what she shared with me!

> I met Vilma when she came to me for help with a distressing problem: she had been belching uncontrollably. She'd seen medical doctors and a succession of alternative healers to no avail. One of the healers referred her to me. Her InnerSpeak* session was particularly scary for me because the more I worked on her, the worse the belching became. I seriously considered telling her that I couldn't help her. But then what I found out surprised us both: Vilma had a past life in China where she had been a member of a healing sect that used belching as a form of confirmation of their work. In that lifetime, she had done something that caused her to lose faith in herself and her abilities. In fact, the exact source of her problem was "feeling powerless against the will of others." Her Higher Self said that what she needed to do was mentally create a bottle and invite the past life being into it, then cork it and give it to God. As soon as she did this, the belching stopped and never returned.†

*Inner Speak is a breakthrough coaching and healing modality developed by Jean Adrienne as a form of removing karmic and ancestral blocks.

†Jean Adrienne, *Conjunctio,* 2020, pp. 11–12.

8

What about the Earth?

Mother Earth will be going through a transformation. She may need to expunge certain energies. Our ET siblings may have advanced solutions to some of the basic problems. They may telepathically present these solutions, or once the ET presence is recognized, directly influence the solutions.

All of the pollution and misuses of Mother Earth, also known as the living being Gaia, will be cleared. Some clearing will occur almost instantaneously, while other clearing work will come through technologies not yet known. Do not worry or fear or fight for things. Instead, keep visualizing our beautiful planet as one that's in perfect balance of both the plant and animal kingdom, overseen by respectful human stewards.

Our next stage of development into 5D, into a whole new creation realm, will have a boundary. Consider this: There is no science to support a flat universe! Mainstream scientists have concluded, "Everything we think we know about the shape of the universe could be wrong. Instead of being flat like a bedsheet, our universe may be curved, like a massive, inflated balloon, according to a new study by the University of Manchester cosmologist Eleonora Di Valentino, Sapienza University of Rome cosmologist Alessandro Melchiorri, and Johns Hopkins University cosmologist Joseph Silk."*

*Their findings were published in *Nature Astronomy,* 11, 2019, Alessandro Melchiorri, Eleonora Di Valentina & Joseph Silk, Nature Astronomy 4, 196–203 (2020).

You are currently being asked to take stock of what you know and what you believe. You are also being asked to clean out your toolbox. We start with a blank slate. To get the game going, the planets influence the energy beaming down on humanity. Humans have tracked this energy for centuries; this became known as astrology. There are many different kinds of astrology but they all follow the same principle: certain planets carry specific energy that influences our actions. I use an astrology calendar like a map or a GPS. I let it warn me of impending energies that are affecting humans. I don't let astrology rule me, however, for like a good GPS, it is a powerful tool for navigation. It's helpful to know when the bridge is out so that you can either find another way to get something done or postpone it until a more auspicious time prevails. Astrology helps us navigate the normal templates of the universe.

MERCURY RETROGRADE

What is NOT commonly known about astrology is that you can opt out. I tell my astrologer friends that I know enough about it to be dangerous. I do this to laugh at myself, because I follow their information closely. However, there are moments when astrology's agenda and mine don't match. When that happens, I do a "work-around." In fifth dimension, it is easy to opt out. We'll get to that momentarily.

Many people have heard of Mercury retrograde, because it comes three to four times a year, lasting for approximately three weeks each time. What is a retrograde anyway? It's when a faster moving planet overtakes a slower one. The slower one appears to be going backward, like two trains going parallel in the same direction, but the faster one makes the slower one appear to move backward. More importantly, what does that mean for me? It means that you get to slow down, review the past, reconnect with friends from the past, finish old assignments, and put aside all the "new" shiny stuff you are presently trying to move forward.

Mercury, the planet of motion, equipment, and communication can affect you and hold you back, causing delays and other issues. What's good about a Mercury retrograde period? It's a great time to clean out closets, or do a rewrite of a project or book, because as you review what you have or have done during this time, you will be able to accurately know the ideal improvements. Mercury retrograde also gives you second chances to fix broken relationships and heal old wounds. Restarting a neglected spiritual practice will be easier during a retrograde as well.

Many years ago, a very lovely man I had been dating reached out to tell me he had met someone he wanted to start seeing. I traveled a lot, and he didn't get to see me as much as some couples do. I remember telling my friends, "He'll be back; he met her during a retrograde . . . this won't last!" Well, I was right and it didn't. He did come back. (However, he eventually moved away and we lost track of each other.)

We can find our way through this template the universe provides us with by adjusting our course; rethinking our hopes and desires, relationships, and actions; and exploring the deepest wounds of our psyche. It's all up for grabs each year! Consult a good astrologer to understand what each is year has to offer, and then use your favorite tools to help you solve and resolve all the unexpected actions and reactions that will occur.

Let yourself be peaceful in this time of uncertainty and chaos. It is time to use your tools, such as the Orion Oil Blends, an Intention Disk, use them proactively. Start now by asking yourself: "If I had a magic wand, what would I do to change things?" "If I had a magic wand, what would I do to make my life perfect?" "If I had a magic wand, what would I do to help myself or the world?" Play this game daily with yourself. It will help you eliminate the old unnecessary paradigms much more quickly.

This is one way you can proactively participate in the creation of your future.

THE WEATHER CRYSTAL

I first met Tuc in Mexico City, on the bus on the way to a Seed of Life workshop. He and I had an instant connection and began an extensively involved conversation, sitting next to each other on the long bus ride to Tonalli. Tuc was doing most of the talking. At one point, he stopped in amazement and said to me, "You are the first person over thirty-five who I don't have to slow down for, or repeat myself or rephrase what I have just said." I thanked him for the compliment. Later he called me Indigo 1.1 and referred to himself as Indigo 1.3.

In the workshop we were randomly paired in the breakout groups in the first three out of four pairings! Another man, I'll call him Andrew, was also partnered with us the same three times. The three of us began to pal around together. Tuc was giving healings to anybody and everybody. I kept checking in with my Higher Self over the next few days to see if I should have a "healing" with him. There didn't seem to be any energy on it one way or another so I didn't bother. On the last day, however, I did get the go-ahead from my Higher Self and arranged to meet with Tuc in the cafeteria at 6:00 a.m. for my healing session. I told Andrew I was having a session with Tuc on Saturday and did he want one too? He said, "Yes, maybe I will," and Tuc responded with, "Good, I'll do both of you at the same time."

We three met at 6:00 a.m. and within a very short time, as we were figuring out what we would be doing, I turned to Andrew and said, "You are not supposed to have a healing." He responded, "Yes, I got that too." "What are you doing here?" I wondered out loud. In a flash I was shown that his presence was needed as a sentry. He nodded; that felt right to him as well. We knew he would be working closely with me, but I had to have someone stand watch. I finally understood that some very high stakes were involved in what we were about to do. It was bigger than any of us thought it would be initially, due to the need for Andrew to stand watch. It was a very big deal.

During the healing, Tuc and I carefully removed a large (three-foot) crystal from my right femur. I placed it into the atmosphere for use. I don't know who else knows how to use it besides me. I had hidden it in my body since the time of Atlantis. It was now okay to be released into the atmosphere.

WEATHER WORKER

Ever since then I have found I am working with the weather. Whenever I would show up in a city, even when the weather was really bad, with rain predicted all weekend, the minute my plane arrived the weather would clear and stay clear all weekend. My hosts would always exclaim, "Wow, you brought the good weather!" I would laugh and smile, never thinking anything of it.

Then one day after about two years of these same comments, it occurred to me that the weather was changing the minute I showed up—anywhere. I began to test the universe to see if I really was affecting the weather. I felt a bit like Superman, trying not to hurt anything while testing my strength. I then accepted the mantle being given me and underwent inner training on how to work with the weather. Initially, I wondered by what authority I was manipulating the weather. My guides laughed at me, stating that their instructions were always about me "undoing" the harm created by disrespectful weather manipulators (human created and machine generated!). (I always ask permission for what I am doing with the weather from my Higher Self and Mother Earth.)

One time at an outdoor family gathering, the clouds moved in. One neighbor and I were the last to come inside; the bonfire we had going was so lovely. She made me look at the sky, and the clouds had completely moved in, filling the sky with one exception—directly above me was a hole in the clouds and it wasn't coming from the fire as I wasn't anywhere near the bonfire.

In another incident at my home I served dinner on the patio and my guest noted how the clouds were so beautiful. Later we went outside, and my friend noted that the clouds had completely filled the sky. This made it look a bit like a jigsaw puzzle or as though cracked, dried-up mud puddles were completely filling the sky. I felt compelled to tell some of my weather experiences, so I did. Twenty minutes later, when we were preparing to come indoors again, I looked up and there was a hole in the clouds, just like there had been on the other occasions!

When my niece was getting married in Normandy, France, I joined her for a walk on the castle grounds where the wedding reception would take place the next day. The weather was terrible—cloudy, cold, rainy—just miserable. I had asked my Higher Self if I had permission to work on the weather for my niece's wedding and I was told, "This is the bride's decision." So I took her arm and asked what she would like for weather. She immediately gave a set of instructions, just like she was talking to the caterer! First it must be sunny and warm—we needed a slight breeze that would dry everything off. And it had to stay that way for the next day as well, because my niece's husband's grandmother was putting on an outdoor brunch then.

The next day was the wedding day, and the weather was still cold and rainy. I did my "weather work" and at 3:30 p.m. it was still miserable. I waited. The wedding was scheduled for 4:00 p.m., and at 3:40 it started to clear. By 3:50 the sun was shining and at 4:00 p.m. you would never have known it had been a cloudy day! It stayed that way until 2:00 p.m. the following day, after the scheduled brunch. At 2:00 p.m. it poured hard for two hours and then stayed rainy and cloudy for two more days. My niece thanked me. I told her not to bother telling anyone, apart from her younter sister, what had transpired between us regarding the weather, for who would believe her?

For a while a few years ago, I felt and saw the presence of Blue Spheres. They have been bathing the Earth with very high cosmic energy to assist our efforts. Think of the parents showing up at the school where the students have been "acting up." Their energies (the Blue Spheres) are supporting our efforts. The blue spheres are cosmic beings who were working in and around our Earth as humanity needed support in our evolution. Their presence was strong at that time (of the wedding) and profoundly affected me, and all of our Earth. Once our ascension was secured, they have moved back into Source. Their presence felt like the devolution of humanity had come to an end, and they were here to ensure our reverse course.

9

Power Tools

Learning from the Lords of Time

We are the Lords of Time. We stand ready to assist you to expand your consciousness and comprehension of time, for us an easy matter, for you quite complex. We ask you to stand at the center of a sphere and see yourself with hundreds of threads reaching out from you in all directions. Understand that sometimes as you shift and change your consciousness all of your threads are behind you like a river. And at other times your conscious shifts again and all of your threads are in all directions. At other times your threads are focused halfway around the globe around you.

Understand that these threads of connection are fluid but your concept of time is not. Until this moment you may have thought of time as linear. You have heard time is not linear or that time does not exist. We say to you this is a misnomer. Time exists in the reality of consciousness as a construct to allow you to experience.

As you experience things, you thread these experiences together into a chain. That causes you to believe that time is linear. All of consciousness plays the game of time. All of consciousness is now preparing to shift how it works with time, and instead of seeing time as "no time," we say to you that you will begin to initially experience multiple times.

So you will have experiences in the dreamtime that shows you in another time or in other multiple versions of time. This complexity may show up initially in the dreamtime as we discuss later. You might see yourself in the road not taken. Time is fluid in flowing like a river and you are simply experiencing it as if you stood still. Time is a series of stills and can operate in many ways. We ask you to take time to enjoy stillness. The stillness will lead you into a perception of time that is greater than your current experience.

You can shift and expand time. You can shift and compress time. How will you do this?

Imagine you are a slow-motion camera. You then can experience your experiences deeper and deeper. Let go of your need to set an alarm clock. Let go of your need to wear a wristwatch. Let go of the rules you follow with regard to time from the world of mechanized time and become one with the flow of Earth time. This will put you in harmony with the Earth and help you to become part of the greater consciousness that awaits you as you expand your consciousness into your 5D self.

We encourage you to study the 5D MerKaBa and to utilize the 5D tools this channel (Maureen) has made available to you. We ask you to sincerely announce, "I don't wear a watch anymore. I have no need to know time. I only need to know what I need to know before I need to know it. The rest will follow." We invite you to bless your experience with time and unhook from your need to know someone's age and other time-related details. Instead, read their heart, feel their energy, and expand into awareness of the magical use of time—to your advantage. No longer can time rule you. When you announced this to be true you can no longer be held up. Let all of your tools shine, assisting you in becoming your most divine self. You will do this in *no* time. I am forever at your service. We are the Lords of Time.

THE LORDS OF TIME

SEPTEMBER, OCTOBER, AND DECEMBER 2015, THE LORDS OF TIME

We are the Lords of Time, ready to assist you with maximizing your comprehension and understanding of the space-time matrix energy. Your capacity to hold this in your field is great, and you need to accept your gift that is in you and moving through you permanently (through the toning).*

The space-time matrix is a flat plane, however fluid. It follows the terrain of the situation and circumstances and can be bent and molded. Furthermore, you can sweep your debris or other unwanted experiences out of consciousness by simply folding time. Your first exercise goes back to an instruction you received some time ago: you must create in your mind (and in 3D, if you wish), a matrix that produces a finished outcome that is already successful.

The Instruction to Fold Time

Imagine a tube, big enough to hold a human being. See yourself in your current situation, and a future one simultaneously. In each of these scenarios, this giant tube surrounds you. Maureen has written about "suspending disbelief," such as when you go to the movies, and action occurs onscreen that makes you jump, cry, or laugh. Your reaction of jumping or laughing is as if you were in the movie you are watching. When you suspend disbelief, you know you are both in the movie scene and in the movie theater simultaneously.

See that you can bend the reality and align both experiences as if each of these exist in their identical-sized tubes coming up from the fabric of time. Fold the fabric so that the two experiences are right on top of each other and flow one from the other. Do this mental visual, seeing yourself sliding from one tube and back to the other tube effortlessly. See your energy as droplets of liquid on the outside of this double tube, like dewdrops that can

*Maureen had been toning before the channeling session.

weave these two tubes seamlessly into one long tube. Do this at least three different times for each desired outcome, along with the toning provided.*

> Time is a way to enjoy each moment, not to bind you into conformity.

The purpose of the toning and the visuals is to help you move out of being stuck in time. Time is a way to enjoy each moment, not to bind you into conformity. You are a cosmic being, and as a human expression of your being-ness, you have the ability to move in and out of time. You have the ability to use your personal wormhole (as in the toning exercise) and to release yourself from the version of the reality that holds you back. Use the toning to unlock yourself. Use the toning to create a new reality. Take baby steps through the wormhole until you attain mastery.

Learn, study, practice. You are on your way!!!

NOVEMBER 6, 2019, THE LORDS OF TIME

We wish to teach you how to work with time and how to manipulate time. First, stop wearing a watch. Second, learn how to begin your day without using an alarm clock. This is a way to unhook from the mass-consciousness use of time. I want you to see yourself in a busy day concerned about the ability to get everything done. See a rope that is stretched out as a long cord, marking off each project on the cord. Coil up the cords. We ask you to see all the tasks that you wish to accomplish on a jam-packed day, lined up to do on a rope, and then see that rope coiled with the node points of action lining up and being completed simultaneously. (Node points are where two time lines come close together and start to travel together and may merge briefly. When these node points become merged or closely parallel, a wormhole can open.)

*You may use your voice to sound tones that come through spontaneously.

One of the members of the Ascension Institute, Jane, had a dream about teaching a young woman in an unfamiliar environment. This young woman was a good student and she was happily interacting with Jane in the dream, which was quite vivid. Imagine Jane's surprise the very next morning while on the subway in New York City she sat across from a young woman who was identical to the young woman she'd seen in her dream! She wondered if her dream was somehow projecting into her future, or was she having some other kind of experience? She was seeing herself in a different time line where her path crossed with that of the young woman. This "crossing" or closely running parallel allowed these time lines to merge.

This crossing of time line has many benefits, many of which occur when large groups of people come together to meditate for the same purpose. Why are mass meditations so beneficial? It is because as they allow for the jumping of time lines via node points. Mass meditations are often set up for a specific purpose, typically to heal the planet in some way.

We want you to know that all the versions (good and difficult) can be within the same time of each other, and that they can be on top of each other. And they can occur simultaneously.

You can also use this knowledge of time lines in a different way. Start with a small project, a small event. Let yourself know that it is possible to adjust time, your experience of time, and your abilities within time. Make a very clear prayer of intention, "I am unhooking from time. For this cycle of the next few hours, I am going to be able to accomplish what would normally take more time. I am able to do this in time, on time, and in plenty of time."

THE LORDS OF TIME

Over and over the Lords of Time ask you to consider that time is a construct. Past, present, and future are all at the same time. This is a difficult concept. Certain (unnamed beings) could put things into the architecture framework, dig it up in the ground, and call it history. Inserting things into the construct affects all memory of all minds.

Even if their insertion is new, everyone remembers it as if it was always that way! History has been altered, and very few are able to report on the true history of the Earth.

This kind of alteration affects everyone's memory since it is in *all* memory.

We know that linear time is a construct. In higher realms we know that everything happens at once. The dark overlay that humanity has been dissolving was inserted over your reality and erased many of your memories. This splitting and merging of time lines allowed for confusion and distrust of the shamans and healers of this planet. This manipulation has made you think that life/consciousness has always been this way—in other words, that the presence of evil is real, and that you must live with a certain amount of darkness.

These manipulations are how various time lines can be rewoven, and reworked, with new insertions, and could explain the Mandela effect. The Mandela effect is a phenomenon that some people could remember when it was reported that Nelson Mandela died in prison, and wondered about their sanity, when he was released from prison, until they learned there were many who remembered the reports of him dying in prison. I too am one who remembered the reports of him dying in prison.

STAY IN WONDER AND LEARN THE LANGUAGE OF THE HIGHER SELF

I point out in the book *Beyond the Flower of Life* that there are five reasons for the neutral response. Many of you may not remember that neutral can be a response from your Higher Self. Neutral does not mean maybe. It always means that there is no difference in the outcome!

You may remember learning to connect with your Higher Self. Think about being in a canoe on a river, with an island in the middle of it. You may choose the right or the left fork around the island. Both are essentially the same. Your final destination is beyond the island, so there is no difference. The five possible reasons for neutral are detailed fully in chapter 4 of *Beyond the Flower of Life;* however, I'll include a brief explanation here. The five reasons are:

1. There is no difference.
2. Ambiguous question.
3. It doesn't serve you to know.
4. It doesn't serve you to know now.
5. It's not in your stewardship.

In the process of staying in wonder, I began to identify the language of the Higher Self. The more I worked with the Higher Self, the more I began to realize that a Higher Self connection has its own language.

Initially your efforts may be around getting an accurate response for yes and no questions. Then you might begin to notice, as your heart opens, that you are able to observe the reality around you in a non-pejorative way. That is, you observe things as "interesting," instead of "good" or "bad." You find yourself making observations that reflect a new nonbiased view: this is a match for me, this is not a match. *This* is the language of the Higher Self.

Knowing this language, you can actually make a mental decision to speak this way at every juncture. When you practice this language, you become fluent in "Higher Self" talk. I remember learning about (the late) Ernest Holmes and his Science of Mind movement that taught us all to "think positively." Many individuals needed to learn to notice their negative thoughts. Decades later it's considered common to remind oneself to think in a positive way.

Imagine you can do the same upgrade now. Decide to speak the language of the Higher Self and eliminate words that carry a bias. For example, "That's none of your business" would translate to "You don't have the password. Or I'm not comfortable sharing that." In yet another example, you might upgrade "That was so mean" to "I wonder what he was thinking?"

Anytime you "wonder" about something you are speaking the

language of fifth dimension or the Higher Self. Wonder is a fabulous tool to keep you curious without judgment. Wonderment connects you with the Higher Self language, making it easier to "be" the Higher Self in action right where you are! When you are wearing the Higher Self garment and you are talking like a Higher Self being, becoming the Higher Self is a foregone conclusion.

> We are the Lords of Time and we wish to speak to you about so many misunderstandings about time and the time construct.
>
> And we wish to remind you that although you know this, you struggle to wrap your brain around it. We say to you, there is no time. There is sequence, but there is no time. So we ask you to think of a ribbon and then we ask you to mark the ribbon with a few marks on it. No numbers, just a few hash marks. And then we want to put a ruler next to it. Now, if you're watching the ruler, you can look for the number 2 or the number 5. But if there are no numbers, you only know that you have viewed another marker.
>
> Time is like the branches of a tree that can bifurcate and move into multiple directions. What this means is that there could be more than one version of a scenario or an event in your life. The more passionate you are about an event on both sides, the more likely you are creating both sides. This is largely dependent upon you. You may not realize it but you are creating alternate versions of the reality every time you decide.
>
> We have been talking to this channel [Maureen] many times about the five possible choices for these constructs: Two below grade, which are undesirable choices; two above grade, which are desirable; and one ideal or Higher Self choice. So even with good choices there are still three possibilities that might show up in your reality. We want you to understand that time as a construct is a way for humans to enrich their experiences, to give them a point of contrast that they can say "before" and "after."
>
> We do assure you that there is only the present time. We also can assure you that the future might be a possibility in your reality or it might be a probability in your reality.

Many of those versions are also bifurcated, as you construct your own thought processes.

The largest amount of energy that you have is available for the present when you are in manifestation mode and you move your experiences to a different point in time that clearly establishes that you have achieved something. You are loading up the potential future with a probable future.

This is why Maureen's system, her genie system, is so remarkably accurate. It allows the individual to move from this version of the present to another version of the present. This is also why she plays with the students and makes them play and says to them, "Who will you tell about your good fortune and how well it is going?" This is rehearsed like a real-event movie, as a present moment. And she will say to the student who is saying this without passion: "Remember, passion is to help you track. Now, say it like you mean it, this is acting class." Of course, everyone does it over with a little more passion, convincing Maureen and themselves to really feel and get into the moment.

We wish you to recognize that, in any given moment, the more passion you hold for any of your wishes and dreams, the more you empower them. We give the explicit example of moving to a time in your future where you pass an exam. You know you're going to sit for this credential. You want to make sure that you achieve a passing grade so you may show you have earned that credit or credential. You create a scenario that looks like this: You have passed it. What does that feel like? Bring into your awareness the very real experience of sharing your joy of having passed it with someone who is important to you, someone who cares about you and who would be just as enthusiastic about your successfully passing this exam as you are. In this way you are doubling up the energy anchors to increase the attraction factor so that the universe is attracted to that version of the reality.

That attraction factor creates more attraction. And the more attraction it has, the more attraction it will continue to have. This is why Maureen tells you to take the time to feel what your excitement feels like. Take the time to appreciate your accomplishments. Take the time to relish in this victory. Please remember that your versions of your happy event, your versions of your victory celebration, anchor this into your probable futures in such a way that other versions of the future carry less and less weight, ensuring the version you have loaded up with your light is the one you experience. A point of physics tells you that the observed reality is the one that is produced. It is a known factor that when the researcher goes to test the particle or wave, their clear intention affects the outcome. How could it possibly be any different for you?

We ask you to take time to contemplate your happy future. You have time now as you sit and contemplate your accomplishments, your choices, your heart's desires. Don't see yourself taking the test or taking the classes to prepare for the test! Instead see yourself sharing your happy news, your happiness with a trusted, loving friend who will share your joy and make the biggest statement that you can share in your mind. When you hear what they say is real to you, you have allowed it to be valid for you, and you will have collapsed all other possible versions of that outcome into one.

Would you like to ask any questions about time?

THE LORDS OF TIME

I have a question about time that was asked by a student in a recent class: "What is happening right now, where big chunks of time seem like small chunks of time? Everyone I've talked to has voiced the same issue. They say, "I'm sitting at my desk, and it's 10:00 a.m. All of a sudden, I look up and it's 3:00 p.m. and I don't know what happened! Is time speeding up or is it an illusion?"

Time is an illusion. You have certainly named that. Your experience of time is becoming less important than you counting time. This so-called compression of time in the universe and in you creates activities and events that you are not tracking, so that you can recalibrate. So the human experience of collapsed time would be more like saying that you might has disengaged from time.*

The student responds, "That was my big question about time, and that makes so much sense!"

The Lords of Time wish to continue explaining that consciousness is moving into what would be called "no time." So part of what is happening to individuals is they're splitting up into what we will call the "no-time zone" and then sliding back down and landing at a different point in that progression. It can happen when you have dozed off—when you think you're working at your computer and you literally are not in your body and are not really noticing that you have slipped out of your body and then slipped back in. The purpose of this is to assist people in becoming comfortable with a linear progression that is different from a linear time progression. This linear progression could be like events that we described earlier.

We also want you to understand that you can play with time if you think of it as a ribbon. Think of this ribbon as being able to be compressed, or let a loop drop below between two points that are very far apart. They can be pushed together to produce an outcome faster. Additionally, the ribbon can be stretched, allowing things to slow down. Mostly what you're doing is pushing the ribbon together,

---

*The transcriber noted an 11:33 time stamp on the recording device pointing it out to Maureen. Double digit numbers are master numbers. The number 11 is joining the secular with the sacred. Thirty three is the master teacher. While we and others enter into a recalibration of the human experience, those of you who are experiencing this so-called time speeding up are actually way-showers serving to bring in a more harmonious and peaceful version of the reality that is overlaid and integrated into the version of the reality that you have been experiencing. This is also why so many of you are finding yourself increasingly peaceful and increasingly calm every day. Even though you look outside of you, you have had the news and other so-called markers of the reality and are almost mystified: "I wonder why that is?" And we say to you there is something very tangible going on, and this is a merging of time lines. It's not necessary for you to have the experience of that big chunk of time as much as it is to allow the overlay of the new version of time to rest and reside within you.

coming out the other side of the ribbon of time of wondering what happened to the rest of that loop? The answer is that you skipped through it.

There's a way to help people begin to understand the warping of the universe and wormholes that allow people to move through the creation and land in a new spot with almost no time lost. It also means that you can create a time loop purposefully to produce a certain effect and turn one aspect of your life into a backward progression and another part of your life, using your wisdom channel, into a forward projection. This is also pretty fun because you might imagine that you can only stretch the ribbon of time. However, you can also split it and have half of it move in one direction and half of it move in another. Take, for instance, the question you had: "Where is that chunk of time going?" The answer is, "It is not going anywhere because it's ceased to exist." So it just *appeared* to go nowhere? Normally in a linear progression one might say, "Yes, it went from point A to point B." But if you create a connection between two separate lines and loop that, the loop no longer exists, only the remaining line.

Part of this is happening because we think we need to know what time it is. In the immediate past, the need for human beings to know what day it is has been exacerbated. In the distant past, going to work produced a certain regularity, and working with crops or working with animals produced a form of regularity more in tune with natural cycles. And the awareness of time was not noted as much as the events *within* those days. Now, because of the adherence to a clock among most Americans and many other Western countries, the *rhythm and natural cycles* have lost their appeal. So, we say to you, understand this too is an opportunity to acquire a new state of timelessness; a new state of awareness that does not require a definition of time. We remind you that time is a construct and it allows you to separate events and existence; it is not used elsewhere. (Elsewhere in the universe, time is not used the way is on Earth.) And we so look forward to continuing this dialogue with you. That is all.

THE LORDS OF TIME

APRIL 5, 2020, SANAT KUMARA: LIVE GROUP WITH MARBETH DUNN AND HER WORLD PEACE EXPERIMENT

We wish to remind everyone we are stepping out of the business of keeping score. No more "I was here first." The Earth itself is taking advantage of the opportunity that was created by those who would have had humanity fail. It did not succeed. It has been turned into favor for humanity. This means that everything that is going to be an outcome in this situation will be highly beneficial. There may some casualties in this particular situation. These casualties are most distressing. However, we want you to understand, from our vantage point, there are many graces coming your way that you have yet to discover.

Everyone who is choosing to accept this "rule of law" and this "harbor in place" is achieving a level inner mastery that would not have been achieved any other way. Those frequent naps? You are actually tuning in and letting the body unwind so that the higher vibrational frequencies can move in and integrate. One of the most important things that we see from our vantage point is that humans have resisted the high vibrational frequencies that are coming in. This was not because they didn't like them or did not want them coming in, but because they were so busy maintaining their status quo. Allowing people the time and frequency to level down a few notches (by sleeping) is actually allowing them to integrate to higher frequencies, allowing them to seek a higher understanding of everything that is happening to them. In this case we ask you to be patient and loving in addition to all the other things you are doing.

This means loving in all directions. This means loving the people you dislike as much as the people you like. It is easy to love the people you like; can you love the people you don't like? It is easy to meditate in a quiet room; can you meditate in a crowded room? We invite you to look at those people that you dislike, those people you hold energy against, for whatever reason. This could be a political figure or a family member you look at and notice that inside of you,

you have become peaceful and because you *can become peaceful inside,* you can become peaceful outside. You must project that peace outward in all directions not just a limited way. In this way you will help heal the Earth.

SANAT KUMARA: LIVE GROUP WITH MARBETH DUNN AND HER WORLD PEACE EXPERIMENT

APRIL 7, 2020, THE LORDS OF LIGHT CHANNELED THROUGH MAUREEN ST. GERMAIN

We want you to understand you are cocreators. This channel [Maureen] has repeatedly said this to you yet it seems that it doesn't sink in; it is not accepted by you. We ask you to step into your power. Command the universe around you, command the world around you. Demand the clearing of dark energies. Demand the clearing of inappropriate chemicals, allergens, or chemicals in the air, and that they be antidoted and rendered neutral in your body.

Each human is different. Each of you has the power within you. You must claim your power and use it wisely. You have been taught (wrongly) that you are powerless. You have been taught (wrongly) that the world is out of your control. You have been taught (wrongly) that you have no ability to use your power, but we say they are all lies to hold you back. Now that you are no longer held back, now that forces of evil have been slain, it is up to you to step into your true power. Do not let another take your power. Your freedom has been won. Your opportunity is in front of you. Now, how will you claim your power?

1. Own your mistakes
2. Own your successes
3. Own your understanding
4. Own your true love and appreciation of your fellow human, the Earth, and all sentient beings

It is so easy to push blame onto someone one else for practically everything. We say it does not serve you anymore. It does not serve you because you are giving up a bit of your power every time you put blame on someone else or something else. Some of this has to do with humility. We ask you to step into your humility by imagining that you would bow and kiss the feet of your archrival—of the biggest enemy that you think you have. The person you despise the most. Blame will hold you back. It keeps your energy locked out of fifth dimension.

All attempts to request or require an apology are your claim that you are better than that person. Your Christian scriptures say, He who is without sin, cast the first stone. We ask you to step back from keeping score, as this also takes away your power and hands it off to another.

Each life has its own experience. Therefore, it is no longer appropriate to compare your life with another. It is useful to compare your life with another if there is something you want to know, or something that you desire to learn or acquire, or gain in knowledge or understanding. It is appropriate to look at another with intrigue or curiosity. It is appropriate to look at another and decide, "I'd like that." Be careful to use your own power and claim your own ability to achieve these things.

When you look upon another with those possessions or abilities or aptitudes with a jealous heart you not only hold yourself back in 3D but you are giving them more power. When you realize you are giving up more power and giving it to them, we hope you will recognize that it is no different than pulling money out of your bank account and handing it over to people for no reason.

We ask you to claim your power. Tune in to the universe. Learn the Higher Self connection with such accuracy that when you command the universe, that command is aligned with the will of the Divine. And it is in accord with those who would benefit from your command. Keep your hearts open, as there is much coming that will disillusion you and disappoint you. Do your own personal gratitude work, so that you can stay in your personal power and claim your God Victory.* Your heaven on earth.

---

*Beloved Mighty Victory is an Ascended Master.

SELF-AWARENESS

Self-awareness is in contrast to being self-effacing. Being self-aware allows you to see when someone points out to you that your interactions with them are problematic—when you begin to realize that someone is experiencing the same event as you, differently than you. This doesn't mean that apologizing is necessary. It means you can acknowledge their experience. Apologizing and being self-effacing at their core seek to keep you in a game of better than or worse than. If you move into consoling, and seek to discover how to avoid the situation in the future, that is all that is needed.

Every one of us is evaluating our reality through our brain cells, through consciousness. When self-limiting beliefs or thoughts enter into our belief system, the reality produces that outcome! Bruce Lipton, author and scientist, tells us beliefs "control" biology! Beliefs not only control our physiology, they also directly impact the expression of our genes. This means that the impact of our beliefs affects us at every level of life. Studies of students in the classroom tell us that students whose teachers held high beliefs and expectations of them actually performed better in studies and tests. Beliefs not only control our physiology, they also directly impact the expression of our genes. The impact of our beliefs affects us at every level of life.

Then when we look at the reality from the quantum view, we remember everything is *energy in motion,* not matter in motion. Take for example the movement of a tsunami. We think of it as a wall of water, but truly it is more like "the wave" at a stadium event. The people in the stands stand up and wave their arms in sequence. Your eyes follow the movement of their arms, and it looks like energy is moving through them. In the tsunami the energy moves through the water, causing it to "stand up," and then the energy moves on to the water molecules next to it. The stadium wave is not moving, the people are. The tsunami is not moving water, its *energy* is creating a wall of water. Energy is full potential; matter is solidified potential.

Studying tsunamis can actually help you begin to understand pure energy. So unlike normal waves that are caused by wind forces, the driving energy of a tsunami moves through the water, not on top of it. Therefore, as the tsunami travels through deep water—at up to five hundred or six hundred miles per hour—it's barely evident above water. A tsunami is typically no more than three feet (one meter) high. Of course, all that changes as the tsunami nears the coastline. It is then that it attains a frightening height and achieves its more recognizable and disastrous form, because of the resistance of the shallow depth.

Fig. 9.1. Understanding the power of pure energy by using the tsunami as analogy.

Now how does that relate to the reality? I have found that nature mimics what is really going on energetically, which allows us to decode our environment and more. After "decoding," one can redirect awareness. Everything radiates from a single point each time energy shifts and moves. Each "pebble in the pond moment" produces its own effect and interacts with all the other pebbles' waves. Sometimes we are afraid to take the next step, instead choosing to ruminate about what we do not have. Because we are afraid we won't be able to deliver our heart's desire, it becomes a self-fulfilling prophecy. Going beyond where we are in the present becomes unthinkable, yet going beyond is what we must do. You can leap over what you want to something beyond it, which will enable you to reach your true target. We don't know how we reached our goal, but it has already been achieved.

Original humans were multidimensional beings who could manage multiple awareness and multiple time lines. Humans could take both "the road less traveled" and the well-traveled one! You don't have to be locked into 3D all the time. We are anchoring in awareness of what it is like to be fifth dimensional. First you notice the similarities, then the differences.

You may recall the experience of a man in my class. He had been using hemi-sync (left brain–right brain synergy training) cd (by the Monroe Institute) in his meditations. One day, as he was driving down the highway he suddenly saw an image of a gold SUV in his mind's eye. He slammed on the brakes. Then a gold SUV appeared right in front of him, pulling out and cutting him off. His braking early prevented a collision.

Another class member tells of a story where he starts his day with a "prayer of protection." He begins his manifestation tale by saying, "The car next to me was totaled. It was a big pileup and the original car that went out of control actually landed just inches away from me." He says, "I KNEW that it was a cosmic event." I know that my prayer of protections kept me out of the collision

As we become fifth dimensional we are recovering our lost tools and our lost codes that will permit us to break through these so-called barriers of linear time. As we begin to understand that timelessness, or simultaneous time, is the norm in the universe, we will be free to use this awareness to get even more out of life. Then we will have the time, time codes, and multidimensionality to expand our experiences and heal ourselves and the planet.

Yes, but why did we create this three-dimensional polarity? It was a way to have two points that can be expressed from within. Let me explain. If you are already everything (i.e., Source/God) you would not expand, as you would already *be* everything. However, if you have polarity, you can create two opposing points and evolve into oneness from there, thus expanding the "database" of all that is. Choose the not-God choice, or the God choice. Polarity is a way to double the creation. Free will is the way you do this. The goal was to detect the God spark and purposefully experience both, and to ultimately prefer the God choice. Can you understand that at fifth dimension you are so connected to God that the possibility of the not-God choice doesn't show up in your awareness as a possible choice? Your love and connection to Source/God is so great that the possibility of the "not-God" choice doesn't occur to you.

ALIGNING YOURSELF TO THE SHIFTING DIMENSIONAL REALITIES

In the first chapter we talked about how important it is to work with your emotions and completely line up your emotional body with your physical body so that you may slip into the fourth dimension. Then, when you line up your higher fourth-dimensional body with your fifth-dimensional body, you easily slip into fifth dimension. This occurs because when you align your third-dimensional expression and high fourth (remember in *Waking Up in 5D* we said that fourth dimension still has polarity) with the fifth-dimensional expression, you are actually pulling yourself through the wormhole (the nexus of fourth dimension). It's as if the fifth-dimensional you is already there towing you in! The wormhole exists like the path to a combination lock: all the dimensions line up and match, allowing an easy transport.

Years ago, I was returning from an overseas teaching gig with a plan to travel from San Diego to Los Angeles the next day to hear a concert a friend was performing in at the Los Angeles County Museum of Art (LACMA). I figured I'd be able to sleep in, have a leisurely breakfast, and then travel by car, with my husband driving, three hours into Los Angeles. There we would spend some time at the museum, have dinner, and attend the concert. My husband had another idea! He wanted to visit the newly opened Broad Museum, since we would be going to LA anyway! That meant leaving the house at about 6:30 a.m. to pick up breakfast and then head out! I thought that was a terrible idea, since I was just getting home from a fifteen-hour flight and told him I didn't want to do it. However, I offered, "I will check in with my Higher Self, and if I am told 'yes' then I will do this." Well, you guessed it! My Higher Self sided with my husband!

Immediately upon arrival that morning, my husband abandoned me to go get coffee. Now, standing in line alone at the Broad Museum, a woman walked up to my "special line" of people who would pay extra to see the special exhibit. She had two extra "early entrance" tickets that she had purchased six months earlier for friends who couldn't come. She offered them to anyone in line. No one spoke up, so I asked if I might have them. She instructed me to follow her back to her line, saying I needed to go into the museum with her and her family. As I was following her my Higher Self clearly stated, "You need to talk to these people." I'm pretty friendly so that didn't seem to be a problem.

As we chatted, she handed me her computer printout for their tickets, saying, "I'm going up front to ask a question; you will need this if we get separated." I looked at the name on the printout, which jumped out at me. It was a long, unusual German name that was very familiar to me. "I used to know a family with that name, but they are from Ohio!"

The husband smiled. "We are from Ohio."

The grandmother chimed in, "Are you Maureen?"

Pat, the grandmother, had been my mother's best friend when they both were in the same industry, back in Ohio! The last time she'd seen me was at my first wedding forty years earlier! My mother was absolutely shocked and tickled when I sent her a picture of Pat and me. It was so amazing to meet someone I knew, that far from home in an unfamiliar setting.

That wasn't the end of the story because now I was talking with "family." (My mom told me later that Dad and Pat were first cousins.) I offered them my New York apartment if they ever came to New York, since I was spending so much time in San Diego! They were thrilled because their two daughters were in school in New York City, and they did need a place to stay occasionally.

Sometime later, I wrote Michael, Pat's son, asking if either of his daughters were interested in a part-time job, given that I had an opening in my New York office. My third cousin Marlaina (one of his daughters) was the best assistant I ever had . . . until she was too busy with school to work for me. Marlaina introduced me to her friend Jenna who was even more amazing! Jenna worked for me for a number of years and delighted me and our other team members! None of this would have happened if I had done what I wanted to do that Sunday morning!

The solution to the dilemmas at hand is found in the legend of the phoenix, wherein we not only trust our inner guidance but know our Higher Self, which gives us new ways of doing things, which often bring us unexpected rewards.

THE LAND OF THE PHOENIX

We must be willing to let go of the old to embrace the new. We must be willing to accept guidance from our Higher Self even when we don't want to. We must be willing to recalibrate and invite solutions that we had not considered—maybe even ones we don't want!

We must also look at disappointment, whatever the outcome, and decide, "The universe knows something I do not know." We must release our fear of the unknown, release our fearmongering about what will happen if things do not go the way we think they should, trust the process, and pray. Yes, pray that no matter what is going on in your life, in your family life, and in your country, you will find a way to pray for the highest possible outcome. Do not pray for your preferred outcome. Pray for the ideal outcome—even if you do not like the idea or understand it. It may turn out to be better than expected.

The number one thing people need to let go of is "control." This is the most challenging thing to master, yet once you do, you will have "everything." Here's why: It is important to learn to know what you want, ask for it, reach for it, bring it in, and move toward it. *Yet* once the *universe* knows your desire you must let go and get out of the way. Let the universe fill your desire the fastest and easicst way possible.

Who would get in a cab at LaGuardia Airport in New York and tell the cab driver which of the tunnels or bridges to take into Manhattan? We expect the cabbie to know what the best route is, even though it may be counterintuitive to us. Why wouldn't the *universe* have the same skill?

The answer is obvious. It does. But if you are so busy controlling things you may not be able to see that. Years ago, I saw a Disney movie, *Snowball Express,* in which a man inherited a ski lodge, but the legal and financial complications turned out to be outlandishly difficult. While he was wrapped up in these troubles, he didn't realize his child had a solution for the dilemma. Each time the child said, "Dad, Dad," the father would respond with, "Not now honey, I'm trying to solve a problem." This scenario repeated itself several times before the father finally in desperation said, "What is it?" The child offered the solution and the father's response was, "Why didn't you tell me this sooner?"

In yet another true story a child observed a too-tall semi that had driven into a tunnel and was stuck, unable to move forward or backward. No one was able to figure out what to do as the traffic piled up! The child asked, "Why don't they let some air out of the tires?" Priceless.

Finally, we turn to the famous Albert Einstein who said you cannot solve a problem from the same vantage point of the creation of that problem. How then do we solve life's problems? We let go!

Let us envision the beautiful world, the country, and leadership we are creating for ourselves!

SPIRITUAL REVOLUTION

There is a spiritual revolution out there—and you know it. You know it's up to you, and yet you don't know exactly how you can make a difference! I will share a few ways you can make a difference in yourself and others. Let's start with language and explore the way you talk.

I make an effort to choose my words wisely and so can you. I've given up the familiar phrase, "I have to . . . " because it puts your power outside of you! Who says you have to "anything"? Why do you let something implied control you? Instead of saying, "I have to pick up the kids from day care" change it up to, "I like to pick my kids on time because it makes them feel good!" "I have to do this report" becomes, "I agreed to get this done—and I need to finish it now." "I have to meet my friend" becomes, "I am meeting a friend for lunch, and like to be on time." And don't give your power away with the phrase, "I couldn't care less." It's drama on steroids!

One time, years ago, when I habitually showed up at 12:15 for a noon luncheon, my friend finally said, "So, when you agree to a noon lunch you really mean 12:15?" That got my attention, and I vowed immediately to not keep her or anyone else waiting! Later, while asking my guides in the Akashic Records about it, they told me that my actions sent the message that I thought I was more important than her! Whoa! That was not the message I wanted to send! I was just trying to pack one more thing in my busy schedule, thinking that my work was important to finish, and didn't take responsibility for a friend being important or for my being late, until that conversation.

Sometimes we use words that everyone else is using, for instance common profanity or jargon like the word *gaslighting.* Do we need to use objectionable blue words? Isn't it about time to clean up those words that come out of your mouth? I know, I know, everyone says these things—but choosing to censor yourself and then learning new ways of expression is a good exercise to relieve boredom and relieve anxiety, and you'll get a boost of energy when you stop using these words! Here's why.

Consider the most common profanity, the *F* word. Young people use it more than middle-aged people, but some people of any age still like to use it. What's important to understand is just like we are choosing to clean up our gender biases, we may as well clean up our gutter language too. And while we are at it, let's give up the alternate *F* word, *whatever.*

The thing is, when you use any kind of profanity you are tapping into the energy that word is connected with, such as anger, rage, frustration, fierceness, and it sends that vibration out of our mouths and attracts that vibration back into our lives.

Yuck.

When you do any kind of special ritual, whether it is drinking your morning coffee, saying the rosary, singing a favorite song, you evoke the energies that are tied with it from all the people who have used those tools to elevate themselves. Now think about the many persons who use blue language to be hurtful, to cause shame and powerlessness. Certainly you don't want to be a member of that club! Have you ever walked into a room where there had been a big argument—and you can feel the heaviness and you start to react to that? You can feel it. We call it bad vibes!

So what else do you need to look out for if you want to keep your energy up? Well, look at those heavy-duty complaint words that keep everyone away . . . *I'm tired,* creates the energy of being tired, simply by announcing it. So when you notice your energy is down, maybe you would ask yourself, What could I do, what could I take, to help me get my energy up? You could also ask your Record Keepers. I'll talk a little more about the Akashic Records in a moment.

In the meantime, here's yet another way to deal with difficult emotions. When you are angry, it is advisable to think about it, take three breaths, and then ask, "I'd like to talk about that, but I'm feeling reactionary. Can we continue later?" This is instead of "I'm pissed off!" And don't waste a coworker's time complaining about a discourteous customer. Instead ask why you always get the crabby customer. You can do this in a meditation, or if you know how to open your Akashic Records, ask your Record Keepers!

THE AKASHIC RECORDS

What are the Akashic Records anyway? They are the energy field that holds the energy of every single thought, action, or word you have ever spoken. They hold the energy of the past, the present, and the possible futures and probable futures. Edgar Cayce, the great American seer, called it the same as the Book of Life mentioned throughout the Bible. It used to be that only shamans and spiritual leaders could access this domain, but today anyone can get into the Akashic Records. This is due to a dispensation that has been granted to humanity to catch up!

Why do we need to catch up? Our humanity has not kept pace with our technology. We don't understand, even with our massive abilities, our impact on the environment and on each other. There is a responsibility that goes with technology. Sure, many people think that it's common sense, but if that were true, why did all the cigarette manufacturers hide the truth about cigarettes? They put shareholders ahead of humanity. Making money was the *only* goal, and everything else was expendable. We see this again in recent times with the manufacture of all kinds of things we put in our bodies.

Learning to open your own Akashic Records takes about the same effort as learning to drive. You can do it. It's easy. There are a few simple things to learn, and then you practice! My book *Opening the Akashic Records* is a literal road map to take you through that process. It's an on-ramp to the highway of the amazing resource that is the Akashic Records.

Why would you take the time to learn this technique? Some of you are eager to add tools to your toolbox for sure. However, the simplest perspective to adopt is to call life a test and with the Akashic Records as a tool you can take the test of life as an "open book" version of the test. You open the Book of Life for all the answers to why something is the way it is, and in the process get amazing advice on what to do next! It is the shortcut to self-mastery and soul growth.

10

Other Versions of You

Other versions of you were explained in chapter 6 of *Waking Up in 5D*, but let's look a little deeper. You may remember in chapter 2 of that book I explained that there was a man, a former business partner who also was a version of me that stole five thousand dollars from me in a business deal. I asked you, dear reader, was it theft? I don't think so. We now see more people teaching the same concepts. From Tom T. Moore's *The Gentle Way* newsletter he shares:

> I understand this is a hard concept to understand, but I've been told you can't have every one of your Earth lives as a "good" person. Like an actor, you are sometimes [going to] play the "bad" person to "balance" your lives. This is for your soul's growth, as keep in mind your soul is on a "fast track" of growth by volunteering for the "Earth experiment" where the Creator of this universe decided to find a way to work with "negative energy"—something none of the other billions of creators had been able to do. We agreed to be "veiled" and not know the true magnificence and power our souls have.
>
> So our soul's goal is to eventually combine and take over for our Creator and allow it to go to a higher level—and again this is something that has never been done in any other universe, as it has been explained to me (this combining of souls). Therefore, our souls need every experience under their "belt" so to speak in order to be able to

> make all the decisions necessary in running a universe. And I might add that our souls are having hundreds of thousands of other lives across the universe in other worlds of every imaginable and unimaginable variety.*

What if, in *every* instance, we are both the perpetrator and the victim? As my experiences have shown, and Tom Moore's newsletter shares, it is very likely this is so.

I created the Triple Mantra meditation to help you bring in more evolved versions of yourself. You can also use the Toning in the King's Chamber meditation.† I recommend you try both to see what you might be capable of, given that the two have different purposes. Remember, you may link across time and space to higher versions of yourself, more evolved knowledgeable versions of yourself, or even a healthier you. It's up to you. Don't give up after your first attempt! Persistence pays off. I have lots of client stories about accessing knowledge from other versions of oneself, and I encourage you to share yours with me.

Have you ever heard that a person's birth experience can be just like their life experience? If they have a difficult time in the final hours of birth, then when they get close to completing something, they could have a difficult time again. I've seen this consistently. The approach we use to set things in motion at birth becomes a template and a form of a contract. You can reframe this contract in a number of ways. One is through the Emotional Freedom Technique (EFT), another is Quantum Matrix Healing, a process where we clear recalcitrant patterns while working with a partner. My organization has team members who do this work for clients regularly, and have amazing stories to tell.

In one example session, a client I'll call Nicole received a Quantum Matrix Healing. Nicole had anger issues that she wanted to get under control. She found herself reacting in one of two ways when she felt she

---

*From *The Gentle Way* newsletter, October 16, 2010, available on Tom T. Moore's website, www.thegentlewaybook.com.

†Many meditations are available for readers to download for free on the monthly blog post, at www.maureenstgermain.com/blog.

was disrespected: either brushing the incident off or going ballistic. She understood neither reaction gave her the results she wanted or helped the situation. When we undertook her healing, her first visual was a rabbit (not wanting to upset anyone), which may have been ingrained as a cultural miasma. The second visual was the tornado, of all heck breaking loose. Neither response was serving her anymore. During the session she was able to resolve the issue and give the evolved response for each issue as it came up. What a relief!

MAGICAL IDEA TO AMP IT UP!

Many years ago I was taught by one of my spiritual teachers that one's birthday is a most sacred day. This is because it is the anniversary of our soul moving into physical form. The most important message about this is that all of the Ascended Masters and our angels and guides celebrate our birthday with us. They have gifts for us that we must claim. Like winning the lottery, if we don't claim our prize, we can't collect it.

As I advanced in my spiritual work, I was using this tool on my birthday, year after year after year, until I hit on an idea. I noticed that I would begin to mention my birthday beginning about six weeks before it and concluding about six weeks after it. This means that I could be talking about my birthday for a total of three months.

I decided that if I had such a great imagination and could imagine many presents coming to me on my birthday, why couldn't I imagine that I had more presents than I could possibly open coming from my unseen helpers as well? It was at this point that I decided I would start asking for my gifts every single time my birthday came up in conversation. This meant I was talking about my birthday (and then using it as a mental cue to ask my angels and Ascended Master Guides for some of my presents). This led to some very interesting results. In the section "Crossing Over and Back" below, I share one of these special requests with amazing results. I've been doing this for over twenty years. You can too! Below is my version of how to use this birthday energy, after an original by Kuthumi, revealed through Elizabeth Clare Prophet.

Again, your birthday is an auspicious day because it is the anniversary of the embodiment of your life stream on planet Earth. Each year, as this anniversary of your soul unfolds, your energy withdraws. This is like a tide going out as you release the patterns, designs, and desires of the previous cycle and make room for the incoming flow of the coming year. This is why the individual may feel the lessening of energy and purpose as their birthday approaches.

Those of you who have enlisted the aid and assistance of the Ascended Masters, angels, and guides will, again, receive gifts from Spirit. These gifts are beyond the scope of human gifts, so much so that you will find that the expression of giving gifts here on Earth is but a faint reflection of the practice of all of heaven, whose inhabitants are ready and willing to assist you by providing for the full expansion, exploration, and expression of you for the coming year.

Avail yourself of this knowledge and marvelous gift by taking the time to ask for and claim your gift for the coming year. As you approach this day, know that it is such a time of honor, gifts, and thanksgiving, making it the holiest day of the year.

CROSSING OVER AND BACK

One year, at a large gathering of teachers who met each year, we were sharing stories of our teaching experiences. I asked two women named Angelique and Christiana to tell me how they'd come to work together. Christiana was about ten years younger than Angelique. Christiana had been getting a massage from Angelique when she (Christiana) passed away. Yes, she died on the massage table! Angelique was pretty shocked and checked in with her guidance to find out what she should do. Her guides reassured her and told her to just sit tight, which she did.

Meanwhile, Christiana was experiencing some very intense replays of prior deaths. First she was being hung, then drawn and quartered, shot, and finally burned at the stake. At this point Angelique could smell smoke! She got up from her post and ran through her house wondering what was on fire! She came back, checked in again, and realized that it was derived from an out-of-body experience of Christiana's.

While Christiana was still "out-of-body," her guide appeared to her and she had a conversation with him. He told her, "Your life as you know it has ended. We have been reviewing some of your more difficult past lives to clean up your discordant energy. By showing them to you you've resolved the outstanding energy."

She responded, "I figured that."

He went on, "We would like you to go back and work with Angelique. She has important work to do and needs a partner, and you are a perfect fit."

Angelique wasn't excited about that idea at all and began to balk. "Well, I don't know . . . I'm overweight, I've got back problems, I've got kidney problems—"

And he interrupted her. "Well, we can put you into someone else's body—but there are integration issues. Or we can fix what's wrong and make it right and the weight will come off over the next ten years."

"I'm still not sure."

Listening with avid attention, I'm thinking, *She's dead and she's negotiating? I want to learn how to do that!* I thought that once you were dead you'd be told what was next. Not that you'd be able to negotiate! (Remember, this was 1996.) She continued, "Well, one of the things I didn't like about being in a body, was that I never knew for sure what I was supposed to do next." Instantly, he announced, "Done!" I laughed to myself, then remembered my pattern for birthdays and thought to myself, *My birthday is next week; I want what she got.* Every time I asked my Higher Self about it over the following year the answer *yes* would always come flooding in, sometimes before I could even complete a full question in my thoughts.

The following year this group met again. At this gathering with the same people, we were talking again about her experiences, teaching and sharing how we were getting advanced information. One person stated that she was getting information about six weeks in advance. Without skipping a beat, both Christiana and I announced, in unison, "Oh, I get my information on a need-to-know basis." I burst out laughing! The only way we could have answered in an identical fashion if indeed I have been given that very same gift, the gift of knowing in advance what I was to do next.

HOW CAN YOU USE THIS?

So even though I tell you to ask for your gifts for your birthday in multiples, and even though I encourage you to ask for what your angels and Ascended Masters think you need, it's okay to make a special request and watch the magic unfold. When I start asking each year, I now also ask for the operating manual of any new gifts I get so that I instantly know and understand how to use them, along with the grace that's bestowed upon me for my birthday. You, my friends and dear readers, are one of them. I'm so grateful for you. Please remember to share this story with your family and friends whenever they have a birthday.

HOW YOU CAN PROGRAM YOUR MISSING DNA

Talk to your body. Even your cells. Command they step up. I contemplated the "lost strands" of DNA that are the self-healing DNA. These DNA strands used to keep us super-healthy for a rich long life, yet were disconnected by beings who were working with the human DNA and using humanity as slaves. They didn't want humans to evolve too quickly. As I began to work with this concept of self-repairing DNA, I realized that this would be the knowledge of youthfulness I had been looking for!

I understood that these strands were disconnected. Cosmic law prevented these engineers from removing this vital force, so what happened? They disconnected them, but that wasn't enough. If my partner disconnects the toaster from the outlet to connect the blender, I can easily reconnect it. They couldn't just "leave them lay" where they would be easily reconnected. Humans would find and reconnect them. Where shall they be hidden? If you are constantly evolving, and you are, where is the last place you would look? Beneath the third dimension! This is why *I command my self-healing DNA to wake up and phase up* to where I am! I might be in a much higher dimension.

I recommend you do this daily. I wrote an evening prayer for you in *Waking Up in 5D.* You can add that to it. It only takes a few minutes to recite it, right before bed.

Humans were intended to have more of our genetic codes available to us, but they were allowed to atrophy and were laid to waste until now. You can now command your Higher Self to locate the Highest Vibrational Frequency (HVF) that your body has *ever* had. Demand that your Higher Self locate it and energize and reattach it, remembering who you are, and self-repairing every other part of your body.

Next, connect to your DNA. Command each of your 64 codons* that make up the full spectrum of your DNA to increase to their highest frequency.

Open your heart to receive the highest DNA activation possible. Let go of your prior genetic programming. Each year I create an Annual Youthing Ceremony that utilizes this knowledge in a ceremony. I do it with a live online class on the Harvest Moon. Building on the ancient African tradition of rolling back the clock two years, I based this ceremony on the idea that on this occasion the full moon is so close to the Earth that it can reach backward a full year, reducing your age two years each time you do the ceremony.

Recently I had my DNA codons tested and I'm thirty-four years younger than my biological age. Even clients from twenty years ago come across my more recent video work and are astonished with the "youthing" I've done. Here's one comment that sums it up: "I went to the YouTube channel and saw a recent video you did. You have not aged a day. As a matter of fact, you look much younger now. What's the secret?" I have not had plastic surgery. If you have known me for a long time and see me now, you will agree.

---

*A codon is a series of nucleotides that form the building blocks of a DNA strand.

11

Spirals and Their Magic

Every living thing is in spiral form. Everything that comes in from higher dimensions is in spirals. Spirals show up in the way that plants grow (phyllotaxis). The spirals allow us to "pace" the incoming information. Everything is moving. New evolution is curved and everything is rotating. Nothing in the world is flat; nothing in the world of nature is straight. Not your arms, not your nose, your fingers, or your legs. Sure, we have straight runways and straight patterns that we draw, but these are all man-made! Even trees have rings! We know that light moves in waves. We know that specific color produces specific wavelengths. We know that smoke rises in curves.

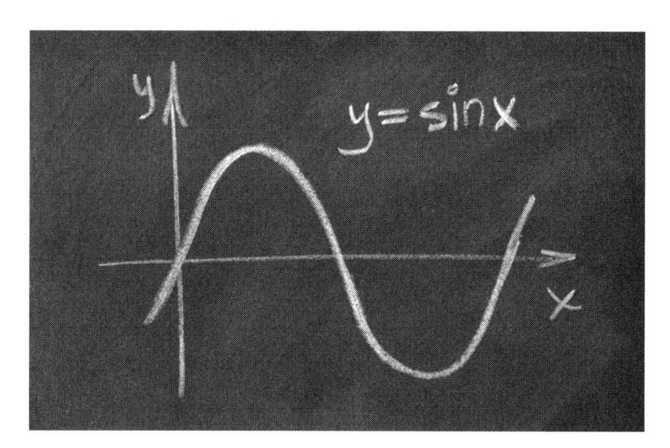

Fig. 11.1. This illustration of a simple sine wave demonstrates how sound moves in waves.

This awareness of spirals, and especially the spiral found in the golden mean, are found throughout the planet in both organic and inorganic matter. This spiral that comes from the relationship known as phi (Φ) or 1.618 . . . hang in there, I'll make this easier. Let's start with pi (π), 3.14, which no doubt you learned in grade school. This is the constant relationship that shows up between a circle and its radius. No matter what size circle, the relationship for the area ($A=\pi r^2$) stays the same! That makes pi a constant. Another "constant" that shows up regularly is phi. This is what is known as the golden mean. This relationship is found in the double helix DNA spiral.

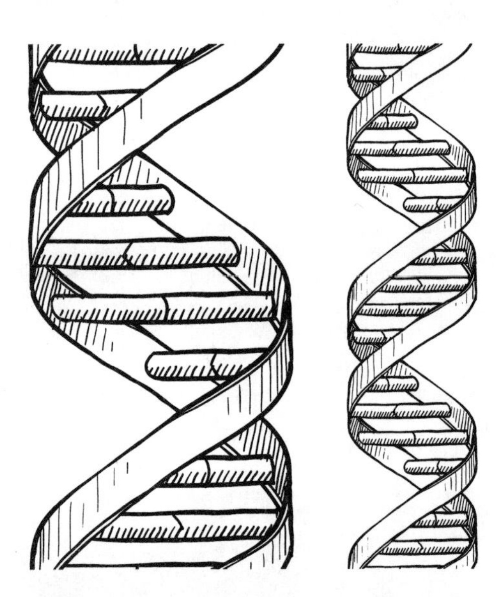

Fig. 11.2. The double helix DNA spiral, which resembles a twisted ladder with its ten rungs.

The measurements used for DNA are units known as angstroms (Å). The ratio between the short distance between the curves and the long distance is phi, 34Å to 21Å. Then we move to the skeleton and find the same relationship of the bones to each other.

The illustrations below feature a tool, called a caliper, that measures the phi ratio. The small part represents "1" and the long part represents 1.618 (phi.) You can see the phi relationship in the relationship of the little finger to the wrist. Next you can see the relationship of the wrist to the forearm. It's true throughout the body. Every part of the body seems to be in phi relationship to another part of the body. This phi relationship is found throughout the universe. We also find all kinds of spirals in the world, for example, the way rose petals grow or the way a spiral galaxy appears. The spiral is a basic form of nature and many of those spirals are in the phi ratio.

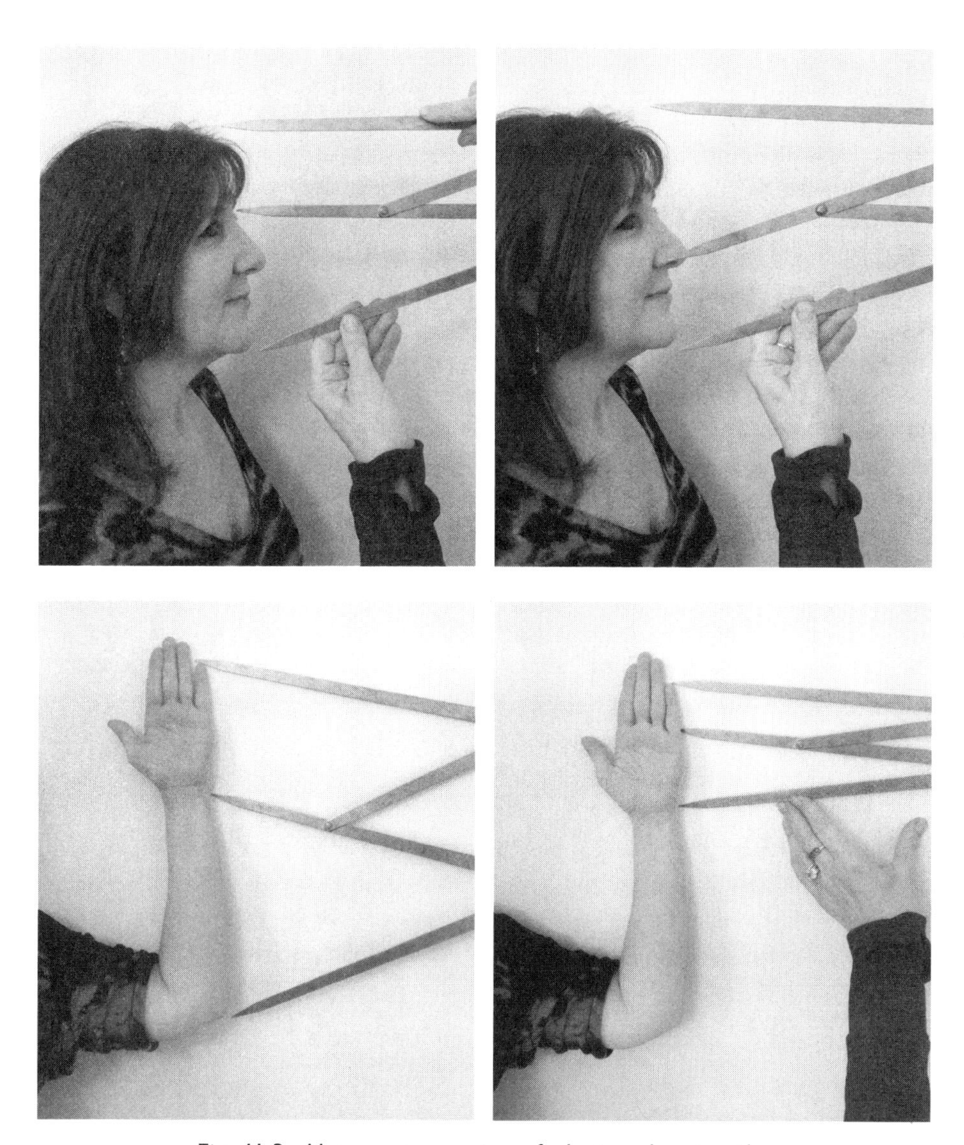

Fig. 11.3. Above are a series of photos showing the phi relationships of the human body.

THE CHAKRAS

Humans are far more than their physical bodies. In the East the invisible part was called the etheric body. It represents all the aspects of the human body that are unseen. It is the chakra system that unites or connects these seemingly disparate bodies.

I was never attracted to the traditional books on the chakras. As a mystic I knew they were important, but could never bring myself to open the books I purchased and learn from the traditions taught in those books. I had an "ah-ha" moment when I happened across a book by clairvoyant and Theosophist C. W. Leadbeater* wherein he quotes Helena Blavatsky, the cofounder of the Theosophical Society, along with a respected mystic from the seventeenth century named Gitchel, whose work I detail in appendix A of this book.

They included Gitchel's drawing of the chakras to point out that the Western philosophers knew about the chakras that early in humanity's development. They mention that they do not know why he had drawn a running dog near the spiral around the chakras, but I did. The "aha" struck me and I instantly understood. Humanity was never meant to have their chakras stuck in their bodies. That was done for safekeeping, and to ensure that they could not be stolen from us. Some basic information on the chakras will help you see what I mean.

First we know that the chakra system is a system of wheel upon wheels. These wheels gather and receive information by reading the (energetic) field around you, and help you know and "read" the field around you. Your chakras serve as an advanced warning system. When something isn't going right, we feel it in the pit of our stomach (the solar plexus chakra). When you see a long-lost love, your heart "skips a beat" (heart chakra). I was told by my guides back in 1995 that our lowest chakra would be the heart. I assumed (erroneously) that the lower chakras would atrophy! But when I saw Gitchel's picture, I knew I was seeing the answer to the puzzle of what I had been told by my guides. Start with the heart. I now knew how important it

*C. W. Leadbeater, *Chakras,* 1927, p. 14.

was and now had the understanding that we must start with opening the heart.

UNDERSTANDING THE MAGNETIC AND ELECTRIC FREQUENCIES

One more thing needs to be addressed, as we approach the spiral system of chakras that is the ninety-degree turn. The human is both magnetic and electric.

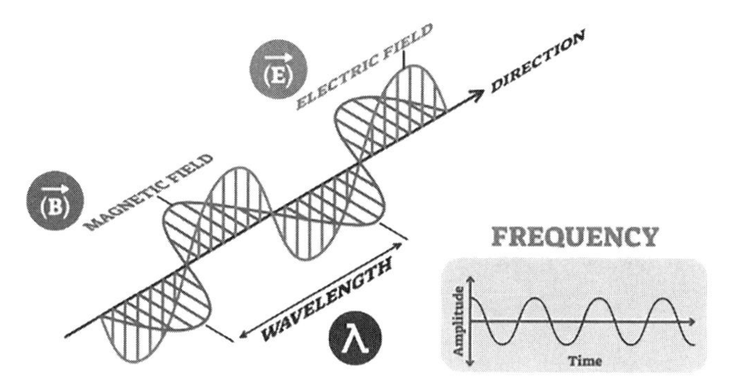

Fig. 11.4. An illustration of electromagnetic waves.

Unless you are an engineer or an electrician you might not know that these are irresistible and opposing forces, making electricity a great mystery.

As shown in the drawing, the two electric and magnetic frequencies are at right angles to each other. The right-angle (90 degree) turn seems to be an important part of the dimensional shift mysteries. What we do know is that the magnetic frequency is receptive and the electric frequency is driving forward action. And we know that the ninety-degree turn allows for a dimensional shift.

Fig. 11.5. A golden mean spiral produced by the phi ratio.

A NEW CHAKRA ACTIVATION

Since 1995 I knew that we needed to start with the heart, and I kept wondering why no one else saw what I saw or knew what I knew. I held this information closely until it seemed like the time was right. This finally happened in 2017 when I met the talented shaman and musician ThunderBeat. She told me that the Mayan elder White Eagle, whom she had been working with on the inner realms, came to her energetically and told her in a very commanding voice, "*We start* with the *heart,*" referring to her CD of chakra meditations, which were presented in the traditional order, beginning with the root. White Eagle made it clear that she was to create a new chakra CD beginning with the heart, and she followed his instruction. Then I came along with more information and now we have collaborated on yet another chakra meditation. With her sound contribution, it's her third chakra CD, this time in cooperation with me.

Remember, I was shown that the heart "would eventually" be the "lowest" chakra of the chakra system. It took a while for me to understand it. This is your wake-up call to what your chakra system could look like. The old system of moving through the chakras in a linear system is based on the linear 3D matrix, starting with the lowest chakra.

The evolved path of activating your chakras is in a spiral, which allows each chakra to be elevated by the one above it, in a spiral just like every other part of Creation! The spiral breaks through the barriers to higher consciousness, allowing you to open and elevate each chakra's full potential.

The Spiral Chakra meditation will start in the heart, then move your awareness from your heart downward (not upward!) to your spleen. You invigorate the energy of the heart into the spleen and repeat this elevating of each chakra with the energy of the one below it. Each higher chakra cleanses and supports the one below it, uplifting it. Initially, with your activated heart chakra, you will spiral down, then up, down, and then up, but think of each chakra in a new way. I never expected to get this information this way, yet it was abundantly clear to me that it was how to create a chakra tool of the highest order! I have introduced it to my Ascension Institute participants for the past three years with amazing results. One person wrote me, "I keep seeing and sensing more and more with this spiral meditation. Love it!"

In this spiral activation you will not be charging up your sacrum, where the gonads are. Instead you will be elevating your spleen chakra, which is also one of your secret ray chakras. Early acolytes never activated the chakras at the sexual centers, but knew the spleen was for vitality, which would receive its energy from the sun. Furthermore, activating the energy at the reproductive centers was considered dangerous by many mystics.* According to C. W. Leadbeater in his book *Chakras,* "The spleen chakra is not indicated in the Indian books on chakras; its place is taken by a center called the Svadhishthana, situated in the neighborhood of the generative organs, to which the same six petals are assigned. From our point of view the arousing of such a center would be regarded as a misfortune, as there are serious dangers connected with it. In the Egyptian scheme of development, elaborate precautions were taken to prevent any such awakening."*

Additionally, your chakras were never meant to be stuck so close to the body. They were initially intended to be like an orbiting energy, not

*C. W. Leadbeater, *Chakras,* p. 8.

stationary! This means you will take the whole chakra system, turn it on its side, giving it a ninety-degree turn. Imagine the two-dimensional model that rises above and below your heart, and then rotate the whole system, creating a spiral, with your chakra centers rotating around your heart, circling your body. They will then move into alignment at the center of your heart. Then your heart chakra becomes both the *base* and the center chakra of your activated system. Each time, you are instructed to allow your chakras to move back into your body at the end of the meditation until you can safely maintain your activated MerKaBa field and continue to grow your awareness of your energy centers.

Remember that the crown chakra is at the top of the skull in the same place as the soft spot in a baby. All the locations of the chakras are depressions, since they were pushed into the body. As you develop, the chakras begin to fill in and expand creating more of a three dimensional saucer shape rather than a flat disc. Your next step will be to allow them to plump up and in the spiral meditation, move outside of your body briefly. With spiritual advancement they increase in size and radiance. This is why the crown of so many Buddhas show a bump on the top of the head.

Spiral Chakra Meditation

1. THE HEART CHAKRA

Put all your awareness on your heart. Move into gratitude. Tell yourself you want to open your heart even more. The first chakra wheel is located in the center of your chest at the heart level and is of a glowing golden color. It undulates and moves and expresses itself through twelve spokes. What matters is that you have powered up your heart chakra with more of your divine self. You love your heart. Love your heart chakra!

2. THE NAVEL CHAKRA

For the second center, we will spiral down to the navel, or the solar plexus, where you can receive a primary boost from the unconditional love in your heart. It has ten radiations. Typically, humans had focused on fear and survival and all their permutations, and this chakra is very closely associated with feelings and emotions of various kinds. Now you will imbue this chakra with love, safety, contentment, and peace, knowing that everything that used to make you afraid can no longer cause any problems.

Although the predominant colors of the solar plexus are orange and red, there is some green in it. You have added more heart energy so that the green element grows. The green allows you to balance the energy that is disquieting or scary and move to a place of no fear and awareness, where all is well. No fear does not mean you go into fearful places unaware. You now take this balanced energy, you know you are safe and loved, and you can express this in the throat chakra.

3. THE THROAT CHAKRA

We now bring this balanced energy into the throat, thus allowing you to express your balanced love, security, compassion, and safety through the voice. You can express this love toward anyone you come into contact with. You can speak the truth with both love and safety blended into it. This greatly amplifies your power because it is no longer scary to yourself or another. The third center you are focusing on, at the throat, has sixteen spokes. There is a good deal of blue in it, but its appearance in the evolved soul is silvery and gleaming.

4. THE SPLEEN CHAKRA

We spiral down into the fourth center at the spleen. It is devoted to the specialization, subdivision, and dispersion of the vitality that comes to us from the sun. This is exceptionally important, as it flows into the heart chakra, which is expanded to hold this love and light. This is also why it is one of the secret ray chakras. It literally is the power center of the sun behind the sun in you. You have integrated much of your energy and now it's time to allow it to spread throughout the body. You have contained within you your own personal power along with the awareness of your surroundings and unconditional love that holds everything in balance. This gives you true vitality, poured out in all directions, including your generative organs but not focused on them. Each of the six outpouring rays carries with it each of the primary colors in their most vibrant expressions, representing the vital forces of each of the seven rays. This is the only chakra that has a dual function of being both receptive and emanating.

5. THE BROW CHAKRA

We are now moving up to your third eye. You are bringing to it your connection to source and vitality. Plugging into the third eye allows you to have a contentment and mastery that would not otherwise exist. This allows you to open to new ideas and be receptive to the connections you are building with Spirit and higher planes of existence. This blending allows you to use your physical discernment along with your spiritual discernment to create a level of mastery, becoming the Ascended Master on Earth. There is much mystery surrounding this chakra. We do know it is related to the pineal gland in a very specialized way, creating perception without knowing how one knows.

6. THE ROOT CHAKRA

The sixth wheel, at the base of the spine, has a primary function related to life-force energy. However, as you have now imbued it with each of the chakras at their more evolved state, your physical connection to the physical body and humanity seems more compassionate and fulfilling. This allows you use to your physical body in a way that makes use of the power, safety, unconditional love, and insight of all your chakras, and permits your whole body to be imbued with your wisdom channel and your awareness of higher realms. Every cell becomes more alive with these energies from the spiral.

7. THE CROWN CHAKRA

You now move up into the crown chakra at the top of the head. The seventh wheel, is also connected to the pineal gland along with the brow chakra, and amplifies this energy into the crown. The right angle (90 degrees) reappears in an important link between the third eye as the pineal emanates upward to the crown. Now that you have anchored all the energies of the physical body into your crown chakra, you have the ability and capacity to understand yourself and those around you with such love and compassion that you "get them" even when they do not get themselves. It allows you to start to connect with the greater consciousness of this reality. The right angle that exists between the third-eye and crown chakras literally pops you into a higher dimension. Because you have added all your chakras to this spiral, the spiral is now moving around you. Understand that this allows you to have that awareness. What you do with that awareness is up to you.

Fig. 11.6. Quan Yin statue at a popular restaurant in Taipei, Taiwan.

EARTH STAR CHAKRA

Next we move to below your feet. This chakra is not connected to you physically but it is there in your energy body. This center is a new center for we Earth humans as we are acquiring more and more knowledge in connection with and in the spiritual realm. These higher realms are part of a new activation that is coming. Those of you who are doing the 5D MerKaBa meditation are tapping into that already. What the Earth star chakra does is integrate the energies of all your chakras that you have spiraled around into the Earth, and puts you and the Earth in direct communication. It also allows you to invigorate both you and Mother Earth simultaneously. This chakra tends to be a beautiful rose with purple, with earth tones mixed in.

8. THE EIGHTH CHAKRA— HIGHER SELF PORTAL

Then we spiral upward again, to the chakra above your head, the eighth chakra, the portal to your Higher Self. This is where you will find the Higher Self, and this is the bridge between heaven and earth. It is the gateway that you widen every time you connect with your Higher Self. It is the portal where your Higher Self energies radiate. It creates an incredible energy. It has an exquisite turquoise and lavender center while the inner pulsation is blue green with red-gold pulsations.

Now imagine you have anchored your pranic tube to both the energies of the Earth star chakra and the eighth chakra, seeing both of them: one above your head, one below your feet. Now see it like a spinning gyroscope, and next take the entire system and rotate it ninety degrees, keeping the heart at the center and letting the chakra centers move around you. Let them sit with you for a moment.

As I have mentioned previously, when the chakras were given to humans, they were never intended to be locked in the body. They were intended to be outside the body where they are far more powerful. Let this feeling grow your awareness of your expansion into mastery.

Stay with this visual as long as you wish, and then allow the chakras to rotate back into their usual place. Feel them lock into their familiar place. Let them enjoy their new direction, and let them see the new chi you have garnered and gathered into these chakras by moving in a spiral. The energy you have created is totally fine to remain in your body. You may feel these chakras moving in your body in this new way over the next day or so.

Gradually you may allow your chakras to be in their new outer location permanently.

Open your eyes when you are ready. You may wish to seal your chakras by moving your hands over them. This energy is far more useful to you this way. One student told me, "I knew where you were going before you did it, and I can feel so much more alive."

USING LASERS TO CLEAR YOUR CHAKRAS

A number of us were at trade shows when this lasering work was being developed and we began to laser our heart chakra with lasers from Vibranz. At first we noticed a number of things, including feeling as if the spine get stronger and straighter! At a class I taught in China, I lasered all the chakras of each of the seventy or so students present. I had dismissed class. Even though it was the end of the day, every one of the students stayed for this ninety-second treatment wherein I lasered each one of them from about six feet away. I was really tired, as I had been teaching there for over a week, yet when I finished, I felt fantastic. I also noticed that I was standing straighter than before! When I shared this information with one of my friends, he thought about it and decided to laser all of his chakras.

One day during the trade show he helped the man in the booth next to him set up his Kirlian photography equipment. As a favor the man offered Joe a free photo of his (Joe's) aura. Joe went back to his own booth, and lasered his chakras as he had been doing every day. He wondered what his aura photo would look like after the laser treatment.

His chakras were aligned and his aura was significantly larger and pure white, meaning he was now radiating the entire rainbow!

We keep repeating this experiment every time we have a chance and get similar results. So look into the amazing potential of utilizing lasers in your chakra work to discover the surprising ways they can help you as well.

12

Who Are We?

Taking all of this in and fusing it together into a way of life and a way of being creates for you the opportunity to be ahead of the curve, not so you may be first, but so that you may help others. Your job is to pay it forward by passing on the knowledge and understanding, being loving and supportive like a parent who delights in their children's growing knowledge.

To recap the foundational principles of this book is to ask you to understand and integrate certain information. You are either a starseed or a guardian or a way-shower. As a starseed your energy is purer than most. Your difficulty is in you thinking that you are human and discovering that you truly are from somewhere else. Your burden then is to step into your higher consciousness so that you *can* see what needs to be done, and then act on it.

Way-showers can be from all parts of the galaxy or beyond, and are here en masse to wake up humanity. You have known so much all along, and have more comfort in this reality than others, even though you recognize that change is needed. You are more patient than the starseed because you clearly "get it." You get what being human is like because you've had so many lifetimes as a human. You have clearly evolved from the human experience and are ready and able to assist the transformation as healers and teachers. Some of you thought you were the odd one. Turns out, the plain old humans are truly the odd ones out—because this is the time and the moment in history where everything is being turned upside down and inside out.

Trust your knowing.

The guardians have a very special role to play, because they are quite comfortable being human, yet have an inner calling to support one or more persons who are starseeds or way-showers. Your job may not involve the "waking up" of humanity as much as it is the support (your physical presence, along with possible financial and emotional) you provide to those who are part of the wake-up crew.

Many of you are from the angelic realm and do not understand why life on Earth is so hard! This is understandable. Being from the angelic realm makes being in a body and experiencing man's inhumanity to man as physically painful. As an angelic you may need to protect your chakras and avoid painful situations, both on the screen and in life. Embodied angels have the most difficulty conquering bad habits of overeating, binging on TV, trawling the internet incessantly, or other addictive behaviors. Yet at the same time you have an unshakable belief in God or Source—and know that God *is*. You can sink really low because you may have forgotten to ask for help from your fellow angels and guardians, both seen and unseen. Help is all you need and asking for it is your "normal" even though you may not have been aware of that until now.

Many of you wonder what the Ascension is exactly. Truly the easy explanation is that it's the evolutionary step that allows more of your divine self into the human self. It does take an evolutionary leap to get there, which is why there are so many helpers here to ensure that this transition goes smoothly. For all of you, the Ascension isn't as much a requirement as it is an opportunity to experience being human and evolved at the same time. You very likely do not need to experience "earning the Ascension" but learning about it. Being in a human body is an experience to be shared and understood, so that you can help others, which is part of your mission.

WHAT'S NEXT?

As we move into this great golden age that was promised so long ago, you will be filled with a sense of relief and happiness. It's been a bit like wondering when your toddler will stop needing diapers! You are so ready for everyone to catch up, and to step up. One day this age will be over, and there will be new adventures for all humanity. Right now, humanity is in the throes of learning that it was all a game. Some of the players got too rough, and the game is over! Staying out of judgment will be your most difficult decision. It is a decision, because you are so indoctrinated with the idea of "lack" and "fairness" that you might not understand the possibly of the absence of a crime, much less an unpunished crime.

Many of you are such high beings that your sensibilities and ethics are challenged by this notion. How can all those atrocities occur without punishment? Their loss is not being with you, not being with Source, and it is enough. Those who fail made mistakes. Those who repeatedly failed chose to eliminate the God connection. Even those who have eliminated the God connection will be able to find their way back to God and full participation in the society if they choose to embrace the one God choice. Remember that your job is not to keep score of others, but to make sure you have taken care of your part. In that way your judgment will lose its grip on you, and you will be willing and able to welcome those who have let you down, have hurt humanity, and more.

We ask you to pay attention to your resistance. Notice your polarity and allow yourself to vacillate. Like electricity that has opposing and attracting elements of magnetic and electric energies, your experience of polarity propels into the next experience and ultimately heightens your ability to enter higher planes of existence.

THE MAGNANIMOUS DIMENSION CHANNELED BY MAUREEN FROM THE COUNCIL OF NINE

I am now asking for a most magnanimous outcome!

We will talk about the Magnanimous Dimension. As indicated by us, we have urged you to bring in the energy of the combined integration of three dimensions. We know you are quite familiar with the energy of the third dimension—its polarity, its divisiveness, its goodness—and yes there is goodness in third dimension. Fourth dimension is integrating now within each of you. You are beginning to tap into the depths of joy, presence, and love. Fourth dimension is the portal through which you magnify and transport yourself into fifth dimension. Because your world has been slow to catch up, we now are offering to you the combined quality of this nexus into the fifth dimension to reach each and every one of you. We name it the "Magnanimous Dimension"—an energy of great integration. It consists of knowing and understanding the perils of third, the passion of fourth, and the ecstasy of fifth, and distilling it into an exquisite elixir of magnanimity.

From fifth dimension, accepting and allowing so much is being magnanimous. There is no other way to describe it! Imagine that you are at the docks of a very large harbor. All the boats that belong there are out at sea, but are still somehow tied to the harbor. Some are closer than others. You have a magical winch you can turn that will allow you to bring all the boats to the harbor. You turn it slowly, gently, bringing every boat into its dock, taking your time, through high and low tide. *This* is the magnanimous dimension—the place of great compassion and love for all of humanity.

THE COUNCIL OF NINE

GUIDED MEDITATIONS

All of these guided meditations are part of you choosing to schedule and plan time for inward focus to expand the higher consciousness of who you are and integrating back into your physical body. The meditations and activations in this book will help you step into the place that you want to be. It will give you the ease you need to let go of your 3D suit and replace it with your 5D suit. It lets you be the grandparent to the toddler. You love your grandchild so much that you don't mind their choices, their behaviors, and know they will grow out of them, so you don't worry about it.

The Golden Time meditation is a very powerful meditation that will take you into the great golden age so powerfully that you no longer worry or fear. Its twelve points of light will help you infuse yourself and your reality, together with those you care about, with so much supplemental energy that you will be unstoppable. Finally, the Spiral Chakra meditation will anchor into your reality the true way of Creation, through the spiral.

We encourage you to work with these meditations to achieve higher and higher states of inner conscious meditation. These higher states will allow you to anchor more light and connection from your higher expressions into your physical energy field thereby elevating you and everyone around you.

The guided meditation Spiral Chakra does a number of things for you. First it moves you away from the very human, male approach into a softer and more feminine approach of working with and activating your chakras. It weaves you back and forth, starting at the heart. It enfolds each chakra with the higher energies of the one above it, instead of trying to elevate the lowest chakra to fit into the one above it. This reversal of the old way of moving through the chakras to the new way, allowing the flow of your energy and attention from an outward and upward expansion to inward and elevated connection, temporarily subdues your physical expression, moving it out of focus for the purpose of igniting your inner fire.

Being in a body causes you to think you are a human. However, focusing your energy on your heart instills your Source connection and your God spark into first the heart and then into the solar plexus. This creates a flowing expression from your heart, moving downward out the back to the solar plexus. It also creates a flowing inward toward the higher chakras, generating a spiral flow that becomes so powerful that it allows you to amplify your heavenly consciousness in every part of your being.

I have always known the lowest chakra was the heart, and as I explained in the prior chapter, the chakras were meant to operate like satellites, allowing you access to higher and higher expressions of Creation. This is a powerful opportunity to take your work to the next level.

SACRED GEOMETRY IMPARTS STRENGTH AND INTEGRITY

In my lifelong love of geometry, and what is now called sacred geometry, I have learned that there is an important role in understanding and utilizing geometry for spiritual progress. The work of Endre Balogh, cover artist for my last three books, is a wonderful example. His art represents symmetry, balance, order, and more. A self-taught artist and former child prodigy (violin) he started creating these mandalas, or "SGs" as he calls them, after a personal tragedy. They now number over eight hundred. I greatly admire his work and encourage you to find symmetrical geometric mandalas that you draw for yourself, or this kind of symmetry that you can look at on a daily basis. It imparts a quality of creativity and uniformity in your consciousness that serves as a framework or scaffolding for all of your creations. It gives you freedom within limits and allows for movement as well as order and simplicity. It trains your subconscious to elevate within order, challenging the very notion of chaos theory and entropy.

PINEAL GLAND ACTIVATION

Edgar Cayce said, "Keep the pineal gland operating and you won't grow old—you will always be young."* Pay attention to the many deterrents to your pineal gland. Your number one enemy, as we have learned, is calcification caused by fluoride. Fluoride is used to eliminate germs and it's in freeze-dried packaging and vacuum packaging. It's also in every dental product your dentist uses! Don't stop going to the dentist; instead do remedial efforts when you go!

Give your body its true opportunity to reset its circadian rhythm by using an eye mask or eye pillow to block out all outside light while you take your evening rest. Take time to walk in the park, getting away from EMF without your phone. This will do two things for you: allow you to reconnect with nature and give your pineal gland a rest from the bombardment of cell phone and other electronic activity that's so prevalent in our daily lives.

Many ancient cultures *knew* that a clear third eye was related to a functioning pineal gland. Learning about the foods, herbs, oil blends, stones, and techniques these cultures used to support these two power centers can help you find tools that resonate with you. For instance, Love is an oil blend that was developed based on these principles by Vibranz. In my experience, it actually will help you stay calm and heart-centered just by placing a dot of it on your third eye. Many tests have been done on the Vibranz products, but this feedback is purely anecdotal. We found, for an autistic adult male, that his anger outbursts stopped when his mom used Love Lotion on his third eye. *And* if she forgot to use it, or if some problematic food started an anger episode, the Love blend completely halted the drama! Keeping the pineal gland and the third eye clear means higher meditation, greater connection to Source, and more mental clarity. Foods that support your pineal gland are shilijit, cacao, and tamarind.

Here's a little meditation you can use to reactivate and expand the

---

*Reading 294–141 from the circulating file collection available on Edgar Cayce's Association for Research and Enlightenment website.

pineal gland. It will connect you to your 5D heart, body, and brain. We will reactivate your DNA to your 5D heart, your entire body and brain. Below is a prayer in command format to reactivate the pineal gland. You may want to copy it and do it daily for a while.

Reactivating the Pineal Gland

- *I NOW COMMAND my Higher Self to reactivate my DNA.*
- *I NOW COMMAND my Higher Self to reconnect my 5D heart, body, and brain.*
- *I NOW COMMAND my pineal gland to distribute my pineal gland energies throughout my body, radiating outward in a torus formation.*
- *I NOW COMMAND my pineal gland to expand to its highest level of functionality and maintain it perpetually.*

LEARN TO WORK WITH THE ENERGY MATRIX

The energy matrix is the field within which humans live. It is the "ether" of old, and the "chi" of the Eastern religions. The energy matrix is the energy around you that you wield (as an adept or master) or not. If you are not using it for your benefit, then its presence is random. How do you learn to master the energy matrix?

The energy matrix is the field that *allows the flow of chi to be captured and directed.* There are many ways humans use the energy matrix. When they conduct themselves in integrity they are aligned with the energy matrix. When they take good care of their bodies and follow the circadian rhythms they need to follow, they create a connection with the energy matrix. Time is not the culprit. Stop labeling historical experiences as the reason. For example, "I didn't get enough sleep therefore I am exhausted" or "My feet always swell when I travel." *It is also possible to direct the energy matrix or to direct energy through the energy matrix* with purposeful training of energy. Integrity aligns you with the energy matrix, thus allowing you to wield this energy wisely. How do you do this?

- Take good care of your body through proper food, exercise, and rest.
- Accept the body's unique circadian rhythms and honor them.
- Heal your emotional wounds with the tools that have been made available to you. (See addendum of emotional healing tools in Appendix B.)
- Practice the match between thoughts, words, and actions—practicing integrity.

These practices can help you gain mastery of your 5D consciousness and integrate it more fully into your life.

Understand that the flow of life is not linear but spiral. Most humans think in linear terms because that is what they have been taught. You may even believe the events of your life are linear, but that too isn't always true. The more you work with time, the more readily you can see the interweaving of events throughout time.

Bless every event as part of pure consciousness creation. Know that you are participating at every level whether you are aware of that or not. Your observations are limited only by your boundaries, beliefs, and habits. Do your beliefs keep you safe or stuck? When you choose to be open to what the world will give you, you will find your way with grace and ease.

"Normal" is a fantasy. There is no such thing. Expect to be amazed, expect to be surprised, and stay in wonder. Keeping a journal of all your unusual experiences will help you stay in wonder. You can even write that you are ready to see more! Humans like to compartmentalize their understanding, and while that may be useful in 3D it is not necessary in 5D and can sometimes get in the way of mastery.

Humans are moving into uncharted territory. All of us are slated to become Ascended Masters. Like a new college graduate, she cannot begin to understand the complexities and wonders that lay ahead of her as she steps into the world of adulthood. In my workshops I sometimes share a story about our transformation with the metaphor, "What do you call your previous wife? Do you call her your ex-wife or do you call her your former wife? Better still, you can call her your practice wife!"

Everything you think you know today could be turned upside down. The goal of mastering your fifth-dimensional self is to become the most evolved version of you, the Ascended Master you. The universe is expanding, so is humanity. At any time you may need to step away from the expansion and find a point of rest. You may stay there for an eternity, or you may continue to expand the creation! Don't let anyone tell you that you cannot escape your patterns. There are no limitations to the human's ability to grow, shift, and change. That's what the God spark is all about.

Appendix A

Other Accounts of the Centers

It appears that certain European mystics were acquainted with the chakras. They are frequently described in Sanskrit literature, in some of the minor Upanishads, in the Puranas, and in tantric works. They are also used today by many Indian yogis. A friend acquainted with the inner life of India assures me that he knows of one school in that country that makes free use of the chakras. This is a school that has about sixteen thousand people scattered over a large area.

There is also the book entitled *Theosophia Practica* by the well-known German mystic Johann Georg Gichtel, a pupil of Jakob Böhme, who probably belonged to the secret society of the Rosicrucians. Gichtel, who was born in 1638 at Ratisbon in Bavaria, studied theology and law and practiced as an advocate. Afterward, however, becoming conscious of a spiritual world within, he gave up all worldly interests and became the founder of a mystical Christian movement.

Being opposed to the ignorant orthodoxy of his time, he drew down upon himself the hatred of those whom he had attacked, and in about 1670 he was consequently banished and his property confiscated. He finally found refuge in Holland where he lived for the remaining forty years of his life.

He evidently considered the figures in his *Theosophia Practica* as being of a secret nature; apparently they were kept within the small circle of his disciples for quite a number of years. They were, he says, the result of an inner illumination—presumably of what in our modern times we should call clairvoyant faculties. On the title page of his book he says that it is, "A short exposition of the three principles of the three worlds in man, represented in clear pictures, showing how and where they have their respective Centres in the inner man; according to what the author has found in himself in divine contemplation, and what he has felt, tasted and perceived."

Appendix B

Your Higher Self Connection

I always provide new insightful information about your Higher Self connection. I've written extensively about this because is it the number one tool in your toolbox and as such, trumps everything else you might have. Your Higher Self is *you,* fully plugged into God. It's the version of you that cares about you, your life, and everything in it, and has access to all the different permutations of life, and family, and friendships, and work, and your divine connection. Once you connect with your Higher Self and have access to it while in your 3D body, you are always able to choose your highest and best good, moving you closer to expressing your fullest self . . . which is the Ascended Master you, or your Higher Self!

So here are the abbreviated instructions. For fully detailed instruction, please see: *Beyond the Flower of Life,* chapters 4 and 5, page 70.

THREE STEPS TO 100 PERCENT ACCURATE HIGHER SELF CONNECTION

Do this for a minimum of forty-five days, which is your practice period. Figure out what your practice period future end date is. If today is March 1, then April 15 is the end of your practice period.

1. Ask *only* yes or no questions. No open-ended questions. Ask unimportant, insignificant questions you do not care about the outcome of, such as "Higher Self, is it in my highest and best good that I take this route to get to work?" or "Higher Self, is it in my highest and best good that I wear the red shirt?" Keep asking new questions (about what to wear) until you get a yes. Ask unimportant questions throughout the day as often as thirty to fifty times.
2. Always follow through on your answer. No exceptions. This is to keep the practice period clear. After your practice period if you decide not to follow your Higher Self it is okay—but you will probably regret it. So do not ask important questions. If you absolutely cannot defer asking an important question until after your forty-five days, then make an exception. Make exceptions rare.
3. Do not use any forms of divination during your practice period. Do not use kinesiology, muscle testing, finger testing, cards, or pendulums. Divination has its place and can be useful but not during your practice period. If you are a therapist and use these methods with your patients, limit their use to that practice. As far as *you* are concerned, you are only asking your Higher Self during this practice period. Do not ask predictive questions such as, "Will the traffic light change before I get there?" or "Will the phone ring in the next few minutes?" These types of questions are inviting your ego to track your progress. If you are tracking your progress, then you still care about the outcome, thus making it important.

Tools in your Toolbox

1. Unseen helpers, angelic realm, Ascended Masters, dragons, serendipities, elemental kingdom
2. Higher Self
3. Entity clearing
4. Clearing blocks (through Quantum Matrix Healing or QMH)
5. Clearing emotions through Bradley Nelson's work
6. Clearing patterns through EF & H (Emotional Freedom and Healing)

7. Free meditation downloads from Maureen's website: MaureenSt Germain.com.
8. Essential oil blends to clear emotional wounds
9. Stones and Intention Discs
10. Work with crystals such as faden and covellite
11. Guided meditations provided

These tools and others that you may know about are important parts of your self-mastery. Humanity has been through a very difficult period in history, and we have much to look forward to. Humans healing humans are our birthright and inheritance. Many of you have brought forth healing modalities, tools, and devices to assist the transformation of humans. My wish for you is that everything you do, everything you encounter, and everything you bring forth will advance our presence and move us into the great golden age. May you have a life of heaven on earth, for you and everyone you are in contact with!

Index